"Bob lives the truths he speaks . . . . authenticity and genuine life in *Simple Gospel, Simply Grace*. A transforming grace for every pore of my being, every moment of my life."

John Lynch
author of *On My Worst Day*
and coauthor of *The Cure*

"Bob Christopher is one of the clearest articulators of God's unfailing grace and how it benefits Christians today. This new book will enlarge your grasp of 'the riches of his grace' and bring you more fully into what his grace offers."

Frank Viola
author of *God's Favorite Place on Earth*
and *From Eternity to Here*

"Bob Christopher humbly and powerfully points us to Jesus Christ as our source of purpose and fulfillment. If you've been longing to lean into the love of Jesus, you don't want to miss this book."

Andrew Farley
bestselling author of *The Naked Gospel*
and pastor at ChurchWithoutReligion.com

"My friend Bob Christopher explains the truths of salvation and our life in Christ in a relaxed and easy-to-understand style. Backed solidly by the Scriptures and examples from his own journey, Bob communicates the message of God's amazing grace in a way that is refreshing and liberating. *Simple Gospel, Simply Grace* is simply awesome!"

Frank Reed
KLTY Radio, Dallas–Fort Worth

"The greatest gifts given to the human race are the love, forgiveness, and new life found in the grace of God. *Simple Gospel, Simply Grace* does a fantastic job of sharing God's grace in simple and understandable terminology with a blend of Scripture and practical illustrations. This is my new go-to tool when I want to share God's grace with others."

Henry Shaffer
founder of Won by One to Jamaica

"Bob Christopher rightly observes that grace is not a thing, but a Person. That's why the message of grace never gets old even though it has often gotten lost. Find it again in this great read."

David E. Bish
lead pastor, Tri County Church, DuBois, Pennsylvania
author of *I Don't Go to Church—I Am the Church*

"Bob Christopher walks us through the life-transforming treasures of a life lived in the power and assurance of God's unmerited favor. Prepare to be liberated from the chains of legalism and sin as you learn to live from the life and promise of a God who will never even *think* about leaving or forsaking you!"

Jeremy White
lead pastor of Valley Church, Vacaville, California
author of *The Gospel Uncut: Learning to Rest in the Grace of God*

"In a world that is constantly telling us, 'try harder,' 'don't give up,' and 'you can do it,' Bob Christopher gives a refreshing alternative through the message of the gospel. This book will point you to the liberating truth of resting instead of working, and trusting instead of trying. It truly is the good news we all have longed to hear for so long!"

Bob Hutchins
founder and CEO of BuzzPlant

Simple Gospel

Simply Grace

Bob Christopher

HARVEST HOUSE PUBLISHERS
EUGENE, OREGON

Cover by Dual Identity, Inc., Whites Creek, Tennessee

SIMPLE GOSPEL, SIMPLY GRACE
Copyright © 2015 by Bob Christopher
Published by Harvest House Publishers
Eugene, Oregon 97402
www.harvesthousepublishers.com

Library of Congress Cataloging-in-Publication Data
Christopher, Bob
Simple gospel, simply grace / Bob Christopher.
pages cm
ISBN 978-0-7369-6272-8 (pbk.)
ISBN 978-0-7369-6273-5 (eBook)
1. Grace (Theology) I. Title.
BT761.3.C47 2015
248.4—dc23

2014042881

Printed in the United States of America

15 16 17 18 19 20 21 22 23 / VP-JH / 10 9 8 7 6 5 4 3 2 1

To my wife, Jeanna...
the most genuine person I know.

Acknowledgments

First, I thank my mom and dad. I'm proud to say that you can find their fingerprints on almost every area of my life. I say almost because all the bad stuff is mine alone. Their support, encouragement, and belief have made a lasting impact. And I'm grateful that Dad is already enjoying what we all long for—life in Christ's presence.

A special thanks to Jeanna for her honest and sincere insights about the book—stuff like "This story is awful. You need to rewrite it and make it better." She has never been one to play games or to hide her true feelings. This is one of the traits I love most about her. And it has helped provide a strong foundation for us to see and understand God's grace more fully.

And there are our kids, Caitlin, Coleman, and McKenzie. I think they are the coolest kids on the planet.

I'm also so thankful for my three sisters, Lisa, Gina, and Sally.

A special thanks to Vivian Foster, Kim Groff, and Jeannie Thompson for their help on the manuscript. Also to Bob Davis, Richard Peifer, Greg Parke, Stephen Simon, Michelle Lister, and Billie Raybourne. I am privileged to work with these amazing people every day.

I first shared much of the content of this book with a group of men I meet with each week in the card room of a local country club. Thank you, guys, for the many questions you asked and for keeping it real. You guys are the best. Also, to my lifelong friends—Wade, Tom, Richard, and Stacy—thank you for standing with me through thick and thin.

Thank you to Bob Hawkins and Harvest House for believing in this project. I am extremely grateful for Paul Gossard and his work on this book. The faith and courage he exhibited during the most trying of times was a testimony to the reality of God's grace. And to Gene Skinner, thank you for making this book better.

And finally, thank you to Jesus Christ, the one who is full of grace and truth.

Contents

Part 3: Freedom

Foreword

Have you ever been so parched and thirsty that when you finally got a drink, you could feel that first fresh, cool gulp revive your whole body? That's what this book does to your spirit. Bob's writing is refreshing and crisp and awakens the soul. His simple and direct message gives you strength when you need it.

This book was so refreshing, I had a difficult time putting it down. Plenty of things in this world are working against me, so when I find something that nourishes my soul and offers a joy I can celebrate, I want to shout it out to everyone I know. Bob's book provides just that kind of nourishment. He writes with a simple directness that makes his point difficult to miss.

Have you ever read the Greek legend about the quest of Odysseus? In one of my favorite episodes, Odysseus had to sail past the island of the sirens. Anytime someone tried to sail past this island, the beautiful song of the sirens would lure the sailors toward the island and onto the rocks, causing them to crash their ships, sealing their fate forever. Odysseus knew the danger, so he persuaded his men to tie him to the mast of the ship and fill their own ears with wax. The men would be unable to hear the song, so they wouldn't succumb to the sirens' call and crash their ship on the rocks. Odysseus could hear the song but couldn't respond because he was restrained. The men were deaf and Odysseus (whose Latin name was Ulysses) was powerless. Deaf and powerless is not the preferred way to travel through life, but it beats the alternative—shipwreck.

I like the Greek legend of Orpheus even better. When he sailed past the same island of the sirens, he began to play beautiful music from his harp. He was the greatest musician on earth. He could play music more beautiful than any siren could sing. The mariners aboard his ship longed to hear the music of Orpheus and heard the sirens only as a distant distraction. Shipwreck was avoided, and an affection for the most beautiful music led them safely and joyfully through the dangers.

Often people think the only way through this life is to live by "can't" and "don't." They think restraint and avoidance will keep them from a shipwreck of a life. The feelings of "can't" and "don't" keep them feeling isolated or torn by what is going on around them. It is the only possibility they can imagine, but there is another possibility. His name is Jesus. He invites us to a love for him that leads to joy and life.

Simple Gospel, Simply Grace beautifully explains this other possibility. Bob's honest and engaging approach offers the sweet song of life. This message is the one that will refresh your soul.

Tom Davis, DMin

Introduction

God's Guy

*The Christian life starts with grace, it must continue
with grace, it ends with grace. Grace, wondrous grace.*

Martyn Lloyd-Jones

The first day of my freshman year of college, I made a vow to God.
Have you ever done that? Mine went something like this: "God,
I know I've been a disappointment to you. Thank you for a clean
slate and for the opportunity to start fresh in college. From this day
forward, I promise to be your guy."

This wasn't the first promise I had made to God. This time, however, I was more committed to fulfilling it. I really wanted my life
to count for him. I sincerely desired to turn my life around and was
willing to do whatever it took. Much like the Israelites, my attitude
was, "All you've commanded, Lord, I will do" (see Exodus 24:7).

I genuinely tried. I left everything on the court in my effort to be
the best Christian I could be. I gave it my best shot. But my best shot
wasn't good enough. My promise was no match for the temptations

of college life. I gave in time and time again just as I had done in high school and junior high. Every time I did, I felt horrible, as if I had let God down.

Does this sound familiar? I've met many people through the years with a similar story. Frankly, I think every human being lives it to one degree or another. It's programmed into our DNA. I like to tell people that we're all natural-born legalists. We try to live for God, but it's impossible for us to do. The apostle Paul described his own experience this way: "I have the desire to do what is good, but I cannot carry it out" (Romans 7:18).

We can't carry it out or even figure it out. I tried for four years to make sense of the Christian life. Every "brilliant" idea I had turned out to be nothing more than the same old fear-based, guilt-driven plotline—*try harder*. And many of the messages I was listening to reinforced this thinking. Ironically, my favorite Bible verse at the time was Proverbs 3:5-6: "Trust in the LORD with all your heart and lean not on your own understanding; in all your ways submit to him, and he will make your paths straight." I guess I didn't see that little three-letter word "not." Everything I tried came right out of my own understanding. No wonder nothing ever clicked for me.

Sometime during my senior year, I gave up the fight. Sin was too powerful to overcome. All my resistance was no match against its deceptive attractions. Jesus hit the nail on the head: "Everyone who sins is a slave to sin" (John 8:34). That's how I felt. Sin was having its way in my life, and I didn't seem to have a choice in the matter.

Here is the sad truth about sin. It promises everything and delivers nothing. I was finding that out.

One Friday night, our fraternity house hosted what was billed as the party to end all parties. All the ingredients were in place—the beer was flowing, the music was loud, and the people were wall to wall. There were so many of us that the floor started swaying underneath all the weight.

In the middle of all the action, a bunch of my friends were standing on a coffee table. It looked like the place to be, so I jumped up to join the fun. But something strange came over me atop that perch. I looked at the whole scene and saw nothing but emptiness. I felt the way Solomon must have felt when he wrote, "Everything is meaningless" (Ecclesiastes 1:2). That was my life—meaningless. Empty.

My dream when entering college had been to become a doctor and buy a horse farm outside Lexington, Kentucky. By my senior year, even that seemed meaningless. But sin wasn't content to steal my dreams and leave me adrift—it also heaped on guilt and shame in supersize quantities. I wasn't very happy or pleased with my life, and I knew God wasn't either. But what was I to do?

Surprisingly, even with all my confusion, I didn't abandon my belief in Christ. I didn't seek answers elsewhere. I knew I needed him above anything or anyone else. I knew the Bible contained what I needed, but I was so blinded by sin and my own human effort that I couldn't see the answers. Just like the Israelites, my mind was dull to the truth (2 Corinthians 3:14).

Then came the gut kick that knocked me to my knees. I got word that a good friend was in the hospital from a drug overdose. Everything turned out okay for my friend, but this got me thinking. Was I heading in the same direction? Could something like that happen to me? Just thinking about the what-ifs, I started to panic.

Several friends encouraged me to attend a Bible study in Atlanta. I had been to it before because I thought it would help me be God's guy. This time was different. I knew I had nothing to offer him. My record was stained with sin. Whatever was going to happen to me was on his shoulders.

I never met the Bible teacher personally, but somehow he knew exactly what was going on inside of me. He pinpointed the source of my frustration. I had chosen the path of trying harder, doing better, and being better. But on a map of the spiritual journey, that path doesn't lead to godliness. I was living proof. The harder I tried to be God's guy, the more I sinned. I was doing the Christian life all wrong. That was my frustration. I fit the well-known definition of insanity—repeating the same actions and expecting different results.

Funny thing—the phrase "try harder" is not in the Bible. You can't find it anywhere in the Word of God. Maybe you believe God is telling you to try harder or to do better. If so, would you consider letting go of that thought right now? It did not come from him. As a matter of fact, the Bible opposes such thinking. Take a look at the apostle Paul's question in Galatians 3:3 (NLT): "How foolish can you be? After starting your Christian lives in the Spirit, why are you now trying to become perfect by your own human effort?" Ouch!

I didn't know any other way to live the Christian life than by human effort. I applied it to every rule that I thought would help me become God's guy—things like reading the Bible and praying every day, eliminating sinful thoughts and desires, standing strong against sin, and maintaining an appearance of goodness. This all made sense to me; it seemed like the wise path to take.

Nothing could be further from the truth. "Do not handle! Do not taste! Do not touch!" does not work. These rules may appear wise, "but they lack any value in restraining sensual indulgence" (Colossians 2:23). I had learned the lesson and was ready for a new way to live and a new path to walk.

James and Peter both shared a wonderful promise in the letters they penned. It is this. "God opposes the proud, but gives grace to the humble."* For many years, I thought I had what it took to be God's guy. That's what the Bible calls pride. Pride takes you down the path of human effort every time. That's the only path it knows, and that was the path I was walking. Maybe you've walked down that path or you are walking down it right now. Let me tell you, the final destination is not a pretty place.

But there is a bright side. Along this path, the failures, pain, struggles, fear, and guilt chip away at our pride. When we've had enough, humility comes along and opens us up to a whole new way. That's what happened to me.

It all started with the most memorable night of my life.

Nagging Questions

I received Jesus when I was 12 years old at a church youth camp. It was my first year to attend. My cousin Steve built it up to me as one of the greatest experiences I would ever have as a kid, and he was right. It was an amazing week from the first day to the last. The standout moment, however, happened the last night of the camp.

I entered Mobley Hall along with 200 other kids, not knowing what to expect. The vibe in the room was almost magical. I sensed something special was about to happen.

The chairs were arranged in a big semicircle. We all had a perfect view of Frank, the camp pastor. He had long hair and a beard. All week he had portrayed different scenes from Jesus's life. I was fascinated. Polio crippled him as a child, but he didn't seem to mind using crutches to get around. He could move pretty quickly, and he was really funny. In one of his messages, he reached into his pants pocket, pulled out a tiny statue, and said, "God said, 'Don't have

---

* James 4:6; 1 Peter 5:5; quoting Proverbs 3:34

any graven images before you.' That's why I keep mine in my side pocket."

But on that last night, he put all joking aside. The message was the cross of Jesus Christ. Frank's portrayal of Jesus's final hours was so graphic, it was hard for me to take. I had heard the story many times in church, but this time was different. My heart was involved. The story was becoming real to me.

I don't know how Frank did it, but I felt as if he were actually hanging on a cross and struggling for every breath. The pain and suffering were palpable. At the end, Frank uttered Jesus's final words: "It is finished!" Then he bowed his head as if to die. We sat in stunned silence.

A few minutes later, Frank broke the silence. "Jesus did this for you."

C.S. Lewis wrote, "When Christ died, he died for you individually just as much as if you had been the only person in the world."[1] That's the way I felt. Frank was talking directly to me, as if I were the only person in the room. What came next was something I could have never anticipated in a million years.

This single truth captured my total attention…Jesus Christ died for me.

Focusing on one thing and seeing it so clearly was not at all typical for me. My mind normally drifted from thought to thought, never staying on one for too long. I got bored quickly, and that often landed me in trouble. On this night, however, I was anything but bored. My mind's eye saw nothing but the love of Jesus.

I didn't know this verse at the time, but God was etching Romans 5:8 on my heart and in my mind: "God demonstrates his own love for us in this: While we were still sinners, Christ died for us." If I had known the verse that night, I would have quoted it this way, "God demonstrated his own love for *me* in this: While *I* was still a sinner, Christ died for *me*." It was that personal, that overwhelming.

Jesus's love revealed my deepest need. It was right in front of me as plain as day. At that instant, I knew I needed Jesus Christ.

This was such a surprise to me. Until then, camp had been nothing but fun. There were nightly lemon-drop fights in the cabin, Ping-Pong tournaments, relay races, swimming...all mixed in with a few serious moments. But nothing like this. And it wasn't like I saw a bright light or heard peals of thunder. Nor did I hear any audible voices. But a keen awareness of my need for Jesus overpowered me, and it was something I could not shake.

At the end of the service, Frank invited us to pray to receive Jesus into our lives. As he prayed, I prayed. Sitting in a chair in Mobley Hall at the state FFA/FHA camp in Covington, Georgia, with my heart beating out of my chest, I asked Jesus to come live in me.

Earlier that morning, I hadn't been thinking about spiritual things. I wasn't praying for God to do a work in my life. It just happened. Christ's death for me became real. It pushed its way into my heart and soul and brought to life my need for Christ.

I didn't talk about this moment with anyone for a long time. I wasn't sure what to say or how to describe what had happened to me. I didn't tell my counselors at the camp or any of my friends. And I kept my parents in the dark for almost ten years. I told them about all the fun I had and that I couldn't wait to go back the next summer, but this was too personal and too deep.

I was much like Mary after she gave birth to Jesus. Shepherds arrived to see Jesus. Once they had seen him, they spread the word. All who heard were utterly amazed. Mary, however, "treasured up all these things and pondered them in her heart" (Luke 2:19). That's what I did. I kept that night at youth camp in my heart for a long, long time.

Here's the thing. From that point forward, I never questioned my need for Jesus. This truth was in my heart to stay. Even when life was its messiest for me some eight years later, something deep down kept telling me that Jesus was my answer. However, as a twelve-year-old kid, I wasn't sure why I needed him in my life. I wasn't asking any of those nagging questions about identity, purpose, or destiny. I was just a kid, content to play sports and ride bikes and have fun with my friends. God, however, saw me as someone who needed his Son. He loved me enough to let me know. That's grace.

I didn't figure all this out until that Bible study in Atlanta years later. But that night at my first youth camp, the grace of God gripped my heart, and Jesus Christ became more than just a name to me. It was my first grace moment, the start of my new life in him.

One Christmas, after I finally told my mom and dad the full story, they gave me a framed charcoal sketch of that camp. I have it hanging in my office. It reminds me every day of that first heartfelt encounter with Jesus Christ.

Eight years later, however, I was wondering how it had turned out so badly. Following that camp, I continued all my church activities. I participated in the youth group, and if you can believe this, I even sang in the choir. (If you ever hear me sing, you'll understand why that's so surprising.) I went on mission trips and helped the underprivileged in our town through a church program called Faith in Action.

I was doing many "Christian" things. But even while I was doing them, I was struggling with sin. It didn't make sense to me at all. The bottom line is, I didn't know what it meant to be a Christian or how I was supposed to live as a Christian. I was hearing stuff in church—just not the right stuff. Based on what I was hearing and my own understanding, I developed a belief system to guide me forward. Unfortunately, this system wasn't based on truth. Here is what I believed back then.

> I was basically a good person.
> Christianity was a self-improvement program.
> Grace was the door into Christianity.
> Jesus Christ came to help make me a better person.

I thought I needed Jesus to help me become a better person. But I wasn't getting better at all. Every step I took forward was followed by two steps back. By the time I reached my senior year in college, backward was the only direction I was going. It should have been different, right? But it wasn't, and I was left trying to answer two nagging questions.

- How can I call myself a Christian but experience so little power for change?
- How can I be so sincere and eager yet struggle so much with temptation?

Maybe you've been asking these questions as well. If so, I've got great news. There are answers. You can experience victory in life. You can truly know the joy and peace of the Lord. You can express the love and forgiveness of God to others. It is all there for you as a gift from God, given by grace.

That's what I discovered. Christianity is simply grace, from start to finish. Nothing more, nothing less. Grace is the believer's way of life. Not human effort. Not rules, or principles, or regulations.

We live exactly the same way we are saved. Paul laid it out in one of the most famous passages in all of Scripture, Ephesians 2:8-9. "By grace you have been saved through faith. And this is not your own doing; it is the gift of God, not a result of works, so that no one may boast" (ESV). We are saved by grace through faith, and we are to live by grace through faith. It's that simple. Martyn Lloyd-Jones put it this way:

> It is grace at the beginning, grace at the end. So that when you and I come to lie upon our deathbeds, the one thing that should comfort and help and strengthen us there is the thing that helped us in the beginning. Not what we have been, not what we have done, but the grace of God in Jesus Christ our Lord. The Christian life starts with grace, it must continue with grace, it ends with grace. Grace, wondrous grace. "By the grace of God I am what I am." "Yet not I, but the grace of God which was with me."[2]

This is what hit me at that Bible study in Atlanta. It was a light-bulb moment for me, and grace flipped the switch. It cleared out the confusion in my mind and connected all the dots. It gave me hope. I wondered why I didn't see this simple route to victorious living before. I will address this later, but I discovered that this five-letter word packs all the power I was missing in my Christian life. Here is the good news for you. Grace packs all the power you need for life and godliness. I'd had that power for a long time—everything I needed. I just didn't know it.

Grace Defined

Let me tell you up front, "grace" is a bigger word than I ever dreamed imaginable. It's big because it's attached to Jesus Christ. Many call some of what I will be sharing in this book the grace message. In truth, it's the Jesus message. There is no grace apart from him. Grace is not a thing. Grace is Jesus Christ himself.

Search the word "grace" online, and this is what you will find. In the English Standard Version, for example, the word "grace" occurs

138 times—7 times in the Old Testament and 131 times in the New. Stop and think about this fact for a moment. What does it suggest to you about the grace of God? I think it clearly suggests that grace is connected to the person and work of Jesus Christ.

Even the Old Testament makes this connection. Remember God's promise to Abraham? On three different occasions, he told Abraham the world would be blessed through his offspring. What did this mean? Paul explained, "The promises were made to Abraham and to his offspring. It does not say, 'And to offsprings,' referring to many, but referring to one, 'And to your offspring,' who is Christ" (Galatians 3:16). The blessing of God is found in Christ. That blessing is grace. This is exactly the point John makes in his Gospel account.

> The Word became flesh and dwelt among us, and we have seen his glory, glory as of the only Son from the Father, full of grace and truth...For from his fullness we have all received, grace upon grace. For the law was given through Moses; grace and truth came through Jesus Christ (John 1:14,16-17 esv).

Grace is inextricably tied to Jesus Christ. When Christ showed up on the scene, his grace took center stage. If we are going to know anything about the grace of God, we need to look to Jesus.

So what is grace? This is an important question. After all, grace is the heart and soul of the gospel message. It is the good news. The short definition that most of us know is "unmerited favor as given to us in Christ." It is this but so much more. *The Complete Word Study Dictionary* defines "grace" this way:

> That which causes joy, pleasure, gratification, favor, acceptance for a kindness granted or desired. It is a favor done without expectation of return; the absolutely free

expression of the loving kindness of God to men finding its only motive in the bounty and benevolence of
the Giver.

Recently, I posted an article on my blog titled "How Do You
Define Grace?" I was impressed by the responses.

- "Grace is the fierce, strong, shocking, surprising, heart-
  melting, intentional pursuit of God in giving us what
  we really need, even if that differs from what we thought
  we needed."

- "Grace is Christ himself! Simply replace the word 'grace'
  with 'Christ' and see how the Bible reads differently."

- "The grace of God is what saves us, sustains us, and will
  eventually bring us into the presence of God when we
  leave this earthly shell. Grace is not a thing but a person—Jesus Christ."

- "Grace has given me permission to stop gutting it out for
  God. To stop feeling guilty when once again, I've failed
  to 'behave.' Grace seems so simple when we sing songs
  like 'Amazing Grace,' but as we live each day in Christ,
  we find that grace is so deep."

Grace is where we stand, live, and breathe. It is the realm of our
existence. It is Christ in us and us in him. Far too often, Christians
think of grace as merely a covering for their past sins. Grace is active
in our present and moves us into our future. I've defined it as God's
work in Jesus Christ to make us spiritually alive and to empower us
to live in this world as his children.

Grace is not only the means of salvation; it is the way of the
Christian life. It's not only the door that grants us entry into God's

house; it's also the way we live once we are in. Once grace starts in a person's life, it never quits. The simple gospel is simply grace.

That's what this book is all about. I invite you to explore with me the way of grace. Here are several of the key verses we will examine together.

- "In him we have redemption through his blood, the forgiveness of sins, in accordance with the riches of God's grace that he lavished on us" (Ephesians 1:7-8).

- "Because of his great love for us, God, who is rich in mercy, made us alive with Christ even when we were dead in transgressions—it is by grace you have been saved" (Ephesians 2:4-5).

- "The grace of God has appeared that offers salvation to all people. It teaches us to say 'No' to ungodliness and worldly passions, and to live self-controlled, upright and godly lives in this present age, while we wait for the blessed hope—the appearing of the glory of our great God and Savior, Jesus Christ, who gave himself for us to redeem us from all wickedness and to purify for himself a people that are his very own, eager to do what is good" (Titus 2:11-14).

- "Now I commit you to God and to the word of his grace, which can build you up and give you an inheritance among all those who are sanctified" (Acts 20:32).

- "Sin shall no longer be your master, because you are not under law, but under grace" (Romans 6:14).

- "By the grace of God I am what I am, and his grace to me was not without effect. No, I worked harder than all of them—yet not I, but the grace of God that was with me" (1 Corinthians 15:10).

- "But he said to me, 'My grace is sufficient for you, for my power is made perfect in weakness.' Therefore I will boast all the more gladly about my weaknesses, so that Christ's power may rest on me" (2 Corinthians 12:9).

Through these verses, you will discover that grace...

redeems you and forgives your sins
saves you
makes you alive with Christ
teaches you to say no to sin
teaches you to live a self-controlled, upright, and godly life
makes you eager to do good
builds you up
gives you an inheritance
frees you from the power of sin
makes you who you are as a child of God
works within you
carries you through the trials and tribulations of life

As John Newton penned in the most famous hymn of all, "Amazing grace, how sweet the sound." God's grace is the good-news story. It is the gospel of Jesus Christ. It is the very thing that will make your life a good-news story.

Part 1

Life

We believe that new life, given supernaturally through spiritual regeneration, is a necessity as well as a gift, and that the lifelong conversion that results is the only pathway to a radically changed character and way of life. Thus for us, the only sufficient power for a life of Christian faithfulness and moral integrity in this world is that of Christ's resurrection and the power of the Holy Spirit.

Os Guinness, *The Last Christian on Earth*

1

First Things First

Jerusalem is the most fascinating city in the world. I'll never forget the first time I saw it. On day five of our tour through Israel, we left the region around the Sea of Galilee and ventured south to the holy city.

The last leg of the trip took us up the back side of Mount Scopus, one of the seven hills that surround Jerusalem. Let me tell you, the anticipation at this point of the drive is off the charts. The road takes you through a tunnel, and then, as you crest the hill, the city comes into full view. Our driver pulled the bus to the side of the road. Everyone got out to soak it all in. I wasn't expecting the emotions. Tears ran down my cheeks, and my heart pounded with thankfulness.

I was looking at the place where Jesus ministered, died, was buried, and then was raised back to life. The realization was overwhelming. I looked at my wife, Jeanna, and my dad. Their eyes were filled with tears just like mine. It was the same for every person who was with us.

What we experienced at that moment was just a taste of what Jeanna and I would experience several days later.

Monday morning arrived. It was Jeanna's last day in Israel. She was to fly back to Dallas that afternoon. The group would visit the Holocaust museum and explore the Western Wall Tunnel excavations, but the day held other plans for Jeanna and me. We were about to experience the most spiritually fulfilling day of our lives.

That morning we journeyed to the center of Christianity. We ventured off by ourselves to retrace Jesus's final steps—his path to the cross and to the empty tomb. This was a journey we will never forget. Our walk from the Mount of Olives to the empty tomb brought us to a point of personal revelation concerning the central issue of Christianity—the resurrection of Jesus Christ.

As Paul wrote, "If Christ has not been raised, your faith is futile; you are still in your sins" (1 Corinthians 15:17). His resurrection from the dead is the hinge on which the Christian faith hangs. Without Christ's resurrection, Christianity would not exist.

This is the sticking point for the critics and skeptics. They laugh and jeer at us for believing such nonsense. But it did happen. Christ was raised from the dead. We believers stake everything on this one historical fact. It is so important to us that Paul boldly asserted, "If Christ has not been raised, our preaching is useless and so is your faith" (1 Corinthians 15:14). The resurrection of Jesus Christ makes up the basic matter, or substance, of our faith.

Without the resurrection, we might as well eat, drink, and be merry, for tomorrow we die. But with it, everything changes. This is the point that struck Jeanna and me most profoundly.

A Journey to the Center of Christianity

Our journey that morning began at the top of the Mount of Olives. When Jesus returns, this is where he will set his feet, according to the Bible. Jeanna and I stood there, taking in the panoramic view of the city. The Dome of the Rock, the Muslim shrine adorned with brilliant gold, dominates the scene and draws your eye at first glance. But as we contemplated the good news of the gospel, this iconic structure faded into the background.

We walked down the hill to the Garden of Gethsemane, the place where Jesus's agony began. From there we zigzagged our way through the Old City to see the places where Christ stood on trial before Annas, Caiaphas, Pilate, and Herod.

Pilate, the Roman governor, was the last person to question Jesus. He was the one who condemned Jesus to death, had him flogged, and handed him over to be crucified. Soldiers led him to Calvary.

We then traced Jesus's steps through the streets of Old Jerusalem and out the Damascus gate to Gordon's Calvary. Gordon's Calvary, or the Garden Tomb, sits behind a bus station in one of the Arab sections of Jerusalem. The rocky face of the hillside forms the likeness of a skull. When the British Major-General Charles Gordon first saw this, he concluded that it must be the place where Christ was crucified. Very near, he discovered a garden with an empty tomb.

The British have maintained this area since the late 1800s. A guide escorted us to the place of the skull. It is startling to see. The features of a skull—the eye sockets and nose—are so prominent that you can't help but think this was the place. No one knows for sure, but Gordon's Calvary provides a strong connection to the Gospel accounts.

We sat overlooking that hillside, contemplating what Christ endured on our behalf. The Roman soldiers nailed his hands and feet to a cross, they pressed a crown of thorns on his head, they pierced his side with a spear, and they gambled for his robe. When Jesus was thirsty, they gave him vinegar to drink. He struggled for every breath. For three agonizing hours, under darkened skies, Jesus hung suspended between heaven and earth. Then he cried out, "It is finished!" And with those words, he died. He had carried out the will of his Father for you and for me. Our sins were taken away by the One who loved us and gave himself for us.

This is the place where our stale, empty lives end. Not far away is the place where our new lives begin. Our guide led us down a path through the garden area to the empty tomb. We walked in and saw the chamber where Joseph of Arimathea would have laid Jesus's body. We found a bench close by. The words from Don Francisco's song reverberated through our minds—"He's Alive"!

This is the story of Christianity. What's more, it is our individual story. Because he lives, we live—not at a point in the future, but right here, right now.

The power that released Jesus's body from death and clothed it with immortality is the same power that is available to us for living here and now. Living in this power should change us and enable us to experience a quality of life we've never known before.

But how? How do we live in the power of Christ's resurrection? How does this amazing, earthshaking event become the central issue of our lives?

Finding the answer to these questions is the key to experiencing the newness of life God has for us in Jesus. Let's face it—most of us are longing for something new and better.

The hope of breaking free from a stale, empty life and experiencing a different quality of life altogether is bound up in the resurrection of Jesus Christ. The empty tomb announces this victorious hope and invites you to experience the power of the resurrection.

First Life

The resurrection of Jesus Christ is the heart and soul of Christianity because it solves our deepest problem.

For a long time, I would have told you that my deepest need was the forgiveness of sins. But that's not true. Yes, I needed forgiveness, but according to the Bible, I had an even greater problem. Consider these passages of Scripture.

- "Just as sin entered the world through one man, and death through sin, and in this way death came to all people, because all sinned…" (Romans 5:12).
- "As for you, you were dead in your transgressions and sins" (Ephesians 2:1).

Sin was a big problem. And it brought a horrific consequence—spiritual death.

Your mom and dad passed this spiritual condition to you. Their parents passed it to them. Follow the trail, and this condition traces back to Adam and Eve. They forfeited spiritual life in exchange for the chance to be like God. God had warned them of the consequence: "You must not eat from the tree of the knowledge of good and evil, for when you eat from it you will surely die" (Genesis 2:17).

Adam and Eve ate from that tree, and they died. Not physically—Adam lived to the ripe old age of 930. The death they experienced was spiritual. The relationship they enjoyed with God was now gone. The life he had breathed into them vanished. They were now fallen human beings. As a result, when they died spiritually, we died with them.

That doesn't seem fair, does it? Why should we share in the consequences of their sin? The simple answer is this: Spiritual death is hereditary. When you entered the world, you inherited Adam and

Eve's spiritual DNA. What they became after the Fall, they passed on to you. After the Fall, they had physical life—their souls were functional. Yet their spirits were dead, which simply means they no longer had God's life in them. That's how you came into the world. Your body and soul were alive, but your human spirit was dead because it wasn't connected to the life of God. You were separated from him and from his love.

Adam and Eve's spiritual death worked its way into their souls and bodies. The damage to their souls showed up immediately after they ate the forbidden fruit. They realized their nakedness and hid from God in fear. Their friendship with God died. And from that point forward, their bodies started to age and head toward the grave. Spiritual death changed everything for Adam and Eve.

It affects every part of you as well. Let me explain what I mean. The day you were born, you were a miracle of life. You were innocent, untarnished by the world. Your parents probably envisioned a life filled with hope and promise. Yet deep within, your human spirit wasn't right. No one noticed at first, but as you grew, this spiritual condition started showing up in your life.

You probably didn't pay too much attention to the early signs. Maybe you lied to your parents or fought with your brother and sister. These are things kids do. But they start adding up, and eventually you start to ask why. Then the big questions about life start to hit. Who am I? Why am I here? Where am I going?

Adam and Eve weren't asking these questions when they lived in the Garden and enjoyed God's life. These questions became a part of the human conversation after the Fall. We ask them because we are spiritually dead. Pastor Frank Friedmann says, "We were designed to live in a garden paradise." That's why we know something is missing; we just don't know what it is.

For my youngest daughter, McKenzie, these questions surfaced

when Caitlin and Coleman, her sister and brother, told her about
having Jesus in their hearts. The conversation happened in the car
as Jeanna was taking them to a school event. They asked McKenzie if she had received Jesus into her heart. With childlike honesty,
she replied, "I guess I have the devil living in my heart." She knew
something wasn't right.

This is the way it is. At some point in life, we sense deep down
that something is terribly wrong, or we feel empty inside, or we
experience an unexplained restlessness. We feel as if God is a million miles away. All of these are symptoms of spiritual death. Have
you felt any of these symptoms in your life? If so, what did you do
to fill the emptiness or to find peace?

One day a man named Calvin called our radio broadcast, hoping
we could help him sort out his life. In the course of the conversation,
he described spiritual death to a T. Of all the problems he shared,
the one that was most troubling to him was a sense of emptiness in
his heart. He had tried everything imaginable to fill that void, but
nothing worked. He turned to drugs and alcohol to mask the under-
lying pain and emptiness, but these substances weren't helping. He
wanted to change. He had asked God over and over to make his life
different, but all his prayers seemed to go unanswered. His struggle
to change led him to a point of desperation.

He was a blistered soul, tired and weary. He told me, "I've tried
to do the right things. I pray for God's help night and day, but I keep
going back to my old ways. Is there hope?"

Calvin wanted change in his life. God had something else in mind
for him. God's priority for Calvin was life itself. It is *life* first and *then*
change. Calvin was spiritually dead. There is only one solution. Spiritual life. That life comes through the resurrection of Jesus Christ.

Life first and then change. That's the process God works in our
lives.

So many of us short-circuit the process. We leave new life out of the equation and focus merely on the change we hope and pray God can bring to our lives. In other words, we view Christianity as a self-improvement program as if God were there to help us better our lives. I viewed Christianity this way. Like so many, I cried out to God time and time again for his help, but nothing changed. If anything, my feeble efforts made matters worse. I didn't know I needed life because I didn't know I was spiritually dead.

Death is the problem.

The gospel offers us life.

Jesus made this abundantly clear throughout his teaching ministry. Listen to his words: "Just as the Father raises the dead and gives them life, even so the Son gives life to whom he is pleased to give it" (John 5:21).

The Case for Grace

The most fundamental definition of grace is "God's unmerited favor." He shows it to us by doing for us what we cannot do for ourselves.

Dead people cannot make themselves alive. In fact, no one can bring something that is dead back to life—that is, no one but God. With him all things are possible. He proved it by resurrecting Jesus. This is what God does. He gives life to the dead. If we are dead, salvation can only mean receiving life. How else could we be saved?

The idea of resurrection seems far-fetched to many. It does today, and it did in the first century. Time and again the apostles were maligned for their unwavering conviction that God had indeed raised Jesus from the dead. The religious leaders arrested Peter and John for proclaiming the resurrection. The same happened to Paul. He did not let the unbelief of his accusers go unchallenged. In making his defense before King Agrippa, Paul asked, "Why should any of you consider it incredible that God raises the dead?" (Acts 26:8).

I ask you to consider Paul's question as well.

Resurrection is the only means for you to have life. That's what God wants for you. It is his first priority. Nothing else can happen until you have been made alive spiritually. That's why Jesus came to earth. As he said, "I have come that they may have life, and have it to the full" (John 10:10).

A miracle of new life occurs every time someone turns to Christ by faith. It happens daily in every corner of the world. Someone dead in sin is born again of the Spirit and is raised to walk in the newness of life. That is the power of the gospel, the amazing grace God pours out on those who look to him for life.

> Because of his great love for us, God, who is rich in mercy, made us alive with Christ even when we were dead in transgressions—it is by grace you have been saved. And God raised us up with Christ and seated us with him in the heavenly realms in Christ Jesus, in order that in the coming ages he might show the incomparable riches of his grace, expressed in his kindness to us in Christ Jesus. For it is by grace you have been saved, through faith— and this not from yourselves, it is the gift of God—not by works, so that no one can boast (Ephesians 2:4-9).

To be saved by grace means you have been made alive with Jesus Christ. Just as he was physically resurrected, you have been given new life.

You were dead, and now you are alive in him.

2

The 180

My dad died suddenly and tragically on November 9, 1999. He was only 68 years old. The night before, Mom and my sister Sally took him to the emergency room. He had flu-like symptoms and was complaining about pains in his chest and back. He didn't want to go because he had an appointment with his cardiologist the next day. Mom and Sally insisted.

The physician who examined Dad that night diagnosed him with the flu and treated him accordingly. After a few hours, he released Dad to go home with instructions to keep his appointment the next day.

Early the next morning, before dawn, something caused Dad to stir. He got out of bed and walked down the hallway.

Because Dad had the flu, Mom was in the guest bedroom that

night. A loud thump startled her out of her sleep. She got up quickly and walked to the hallway. Dad was lying on the floor motionless.

She knew. As she stood there over his body, the darkness of death engulfed her.

It hurts to think about what that moment was like for her. For the first time in 43 years, she was alone. Forty-three years of life and love and struggle and dreams and hopes and victories and joy unraveled as she stared into Dad's face.

She pushed through the paralyzing emotions. She called 911 and then my sister Gina. Gina's husband, Scott, jumped out of bed and raced to my parents' house to help.

The ambulance arrived. The medics assessed the situation and began to administer CPR. Then they loaded him into the ambulance and sped away to the hospital. They took him to the same emergency room he visited the night before. Upon arrival, the emergency team swarmed around Dad to do everything they could to bring him back.

Twenty minutes later, they pronounced him dead.

My sister Lisa called to tell me the news. My household was sound asleep when the phone rang. When I picked up the phone and heard Lisa's voice, I knew the news wasn't good. Her words still rattle in my head today—"He didn't make it." I started to cry uncontrollably. I could barely get the words out to tell Jeanna what had happened.

My son, Coleman, was five at the time. He heard me crying. He came into our bedroom, jumped into the bed, and hugged me. "It will be okay, Daddy. It will be okay." I didn't want him to let me go. I felt lost. I kept thinking, "What am I supposed to do now?"

Jeanna worked out all the details to get us from Dallas to Atlanta. Before we left, I spent time with the ministry team. They prayed with me and assured me all the bases would be covered for the radio broadcast.

After what seemed an eternity, we made it to Mom and Dad's house. When I saw Mom, my heart melted. My sisters were there with her. We hugged and cried, and we hurt together. We felt helpless. There was nothing we could do. Dad was gone.

We wanted him back. I wanted him back. I wasn't ready to say goodbye. I wanted nothing more than to bring my dad back to life. But I was powerless and helpless. I loved and respected him deeply, but that was not enough to put life back into his body.

The day after Dad died, the funeral home held a visitation. Dad's body was lying in a casket. The funeral home director led the family into the chapel to see him. This was the most difficult part for me. The finality of it all overwhelmed me. We knew Dad was with Jesus. There was no doubt in any of our minds about that. His relationship with Christ was rich and deep. He knew God's love and forgiveness and shared his life. This truth was our anchor in the storm.

Friends and family helped us through those hard days as well. Tom, Richard, and Wade, my lifelong friends, walked alongside me. I will be forever grateful to them for being there for me.

The funeral and burial were held the next day. More tears. Dad loved Mom so much. He loved me and Lisa and Gina and Sally. He was our rock. My aunt Mable said, "God broke the mold after he made Chris Christopher." He was quite the man—gentle, humble, confident, and strong in the Lord.

He died way too soon. We miss him. I miss him. In my desk, I have several pictures of Mom and Dad. Almost weekly, I take them out to see his smile and remember. Each time I do, I think about the day he died. When I think about his death, I think about Paul's words to the Ephesians, "It is by grace you have been saved through faith—and this is not from yourselves, it is the gift of God" (Ephesians 2:8).

Dad's death helped me see spiritual death more clearly and understand why grace is the only means of salvation. It also compelled me to wrestle with the idea of faith. Salvation is by grace through faith. What does that faith look like?

I Was Wrong

As I told you, when I was in college, I had it all wrong about Christianity. I looked at it as a self-improvement program. I needed Jesus to help me along that path. This thought is prevalent in the West and particularly in the United States. Life is pretty good here. We are free to pursue happiness and live out our dreams. Christianity is deeply woven into the fabric of our culture, but often only as an ideology that enriches our way of life. We look to God to improve our current situation and to make our lives better. If we live by his rules and regulations and follow his principles, everything will work out fine. This is what I believed. Christianity was my self-improvement plan.

When I started reading the Bible in earnest, I discovered I was in good company. Before Paul met Christ, he had it all wrong as well. Not just a little wrong—he missed God's purpose and plan altogether.

It doesn't make sense that he was so far off the mark. He was a Pharisee, born of the tribe of Benjamin, a Hebrew of Hebrews. He was faultless as to legalistic righteousness. He was zealous for Judaism. He was tabbed as a rising star among his peers, a leader among leaders. With this pedigree, God's purposes should have been clear to him. However, he was so far afield, he considered the murder of Stephen a godly act.

His thinking did not line up at all with God's perspective. He knew the Old Testament Scriptures but missed the Author of those

Scriptures. He embraced the law but was totally at odds with its intended purpose. He was a staunch apologist for the Jewish way of life but was blind to the real blessing of being a descendant of Abraham.

He was like many of the Israelites in the Exodus. The writer of Hebrews explained their situation: "We also have had the good news proclaimed to us, just as they did; but the message they heard was of no value to them, because they did not share the faith of those who obeyed" (Hebrews 4:2). Paul heard the message, but he didn't combine it with faith. He was too busy building a name for himself. He was too preoccupied with being the best Pharisee he could be. He was too focused on fulfilling the law and carrying out the Jewish way of life. He was too obsessed with earning a righteous standing before God (Philippians 3:9) and eternal life (Romans 7:10). Like the other Pharisees, Paul was diligently studying the Scriptures because he thought in them he would possess eternal life (John 5:39).

Paul needed his mind changed. He needed to repent. Repentance is an aspect of faith. To repent is to change one's mind.

Here is how it happened for Paul. While traveling on the road to Damascus, a blinding light stopped him dead in his tracks. He heard a voice from heaven say, "Saul, Saul, why do you persecute me?"

Paul responded, "Who are you, Lord?"

"I am Jesus, whom you are persecuting."

For Paul, this was a moment of clarity. The plan of God and the will of God was now fully in focus. Jesus was not a renegade, intent on destroying Judaism and everything Paul stood for. No, Jesus was both Lord and God. He turned Paul from unbelief to belief. Paul experienced a complete 180-degree turn. His commitment to preach Jesus to the Gentiles was so radical that he quit using his Hebrew name (Saul) and began using the Greek version (Paul). He embraced his new identity.

Here is what we need to take from this story. Grace moves our thoughts and beliefs to the right place and to the right person. This is repentance. It happens when God opens our eyes to Jesus and we turn to him. Grace initiates this process by directing us to Jesus, but eventually, grace shows us something about ourselves as well.

Paul's conversion was extraordinary. I would love to hear him tell the story. It's a "wow" event from start to finish. What happened was so radical that five days after his conversion, Paul "began to preach in the synagogue that Jesus is the Son of God" (Acts 9:20). But that preaching assignment was short-lived. Paul had a lot to learn. God sent him to the Arabian Desert, where I believe he discovered the truth about himself and the "why" of repentance.

When he was journeying to Damascus, he was not aware of his spiritual condition. He did not know he was spiritually dead. He learned that after coming to know Jesus Christ. Ironically, God used the law to teach Paul the truth.

> Once I was alive apart from law; but when the commandment came, sin sprang to life and I died. I found that the very commandment that was intended to bring life actually brought death. For sin, seizing the opportunity afforded by the commandment, deceived me, and through the commandment put me to death (Romans 7:9-11).

Paul thought he was okay in God's eyes. He believed he was basically a good person. That was before he looked intently into God's law. When he did, sin sprang to life, and Paul died. Sin, through the commandment, put him to death. God opened his eyes to his true spiritual condition apart from Christ.

To the Corinthians, Paul put it this way: "He has made us

competent as ministers of a new covenant—not of the letter but of the Spirit; for the letter kills, but the Spirit gives life" (2 Corinthians 3:6). The law serves as a ministry of death.

This gets us right back to the gospel—the death, burial, and resurrection of Jesus Christ.

Notice where the good-news story starts. Death is the lead, the first chapter. Apart from death, there is no resurrection.

Remember, Jesus came that you might have life and have it to the full (John 10:10). You can't experience his life to the full if you are still holding on to your old life. There's only one reason you would hold on to that old life—because you think it has value. You still believe there's hope that you can make it better. But that's not real hope. That's simply wishful thinking.

Let God change your mind fully. You know you're there when you see your spiritual death as the beginning of your good-news story. At that point, human effort is of no value. You can't change death. That is well beyond your capabilities. There is nothing you can do to change that condition. Just like with my dad, as much as we wanted him back, there was nothing we could do to make him live again. There is nothing you can do to get yourself out of your spiritual casket.

This is a good place to be, but it's also frightening. At this point the only thing you can do is to put all that you are and all that you will ever be in God's hands. This is called faith. This step of faith is the most courageous step you will ever take.

Let Paul help you along this journey. He embraced his spiritual death. He saw his helplessness and his hopelessness. He let go of his self-effort. He let go of his self-righteousness. He let go of his status as a Pharisee. His mind fully embraced the plan of God. He was on board. Repentance was in full force in his life.

> Through the law I died to the law so that I might live for
> God. I have been crucified with Christ and I no longer
> live, but Christ lives in me. The life I live in the body, I
> live by faith in the Son of God, who loved me and gave
> himself for me (Galatians 2:19-20).

Paul's 180 is a sterling example to us all of the amazing power
of God's grace. Jesus's love and mercy turned a blasphemer into a
preacher, changed an enemy into a friend, and transformed the chief
of sinners into a saint. This is the power of the gospel.

This power was on full display in one of the last miracles Jesus
performed before his death.

A Happy Ending

This miracle took place in the little village of Bethany, the home
of Mary, Martha, and Lazarus. John 11 recounts the story. John
begins, "Now a man named Lazarus was sick." He was so sick, his
sisters, Mary and Martha, sent word to Jesus.

When Jesus got the message, he said, "This sickness will not end
in death. No, it is for God's glory so that God's Son may be glori-
fied through it." Now, what happens next is a little strange—Jesus
decided to stay where he was two more days.

After the two days, he tells his disciples that Lazarus is dead and
then says, "And for your sake I am glad I was not there, so that you
may believe."

Finally, Jesus and his disciples traveled to Bethany. When they
arrived, Lazarus had been in the tomb four days. That's significant
because after three days the body would have started to decompose.
So time has passed and the situation has changed since Mary and
Martha sent for Jesus.

When Martha heard that Jesus was coming, she went to meet
him, but Mary remained seated in the house.

Martha said to Jesus, "Lord, if you had been here, my brother would not have died." Martha and Mary had been with Jesus and seen many of the miracles he performed. They saw him feed the 5000 and heal a blind man. They were expecting a miracle for their brother. Their hopes were high.

When Lazarus died, their hopes came crashing down. Like Paul the Pharisee, Mary and Martha did not know the plan of God. Lazarus coming back to life was not a possibility in their minds. Their faith and hope stopped at the entrance to Lazarus's tomb. Once he died, it never crossed their minds that there was a happy ending to their story, that they would get Lazarus back.

Jesus said to Martha, "I am the resurrection and the life. The one who believes in me will live, even though they die; and whoever lives by believing in me will never die" (verses 25-26).

Then he asked her, "Do you believe this?" Think about this question. What was Jesus asking Martha? What is he asking us? The gravity of the question did not register with Martha. She said to him, "Yes, Lord. I believe that you are the Messiah, the Son of God, who is to come into the world." She didn't answer his question. But she did go get Mary.

Mary went outside the village to where Jesus was. She fell at his feet saying to him, "Lord, if you had been here, my brother would not have died."

> When Jesus saw her weeping, and the Jews who had come along with her also weeping, he was deeply moved in spirit and troubled. "Where have you laid him?" he asked.
>
> "Come and see, Lord," they replied.
>
> Jesus wept.
>
> Then the Jews said, "See how he loved him!"

But some of them said, "Could not he who opened
the eyes of the blind man also have kept this man from
dying?" (verses 33-37).

Martha, Mary, and the entire group of mourners were all saying, "Jesus could have done something before Lazarus died." What
is the implication? It is this. They did not believe Jesus had power
over death. They did not believe he could bring Lazarus back to life.
Once Lazarus died, their hope for a miracle vanished.

Jesus proved otherwise.

> They took away the stone. Then Jesus looked up and said,
> "Father, I thank you that you have heard me. I knew that
> you always hear me, but I said this for the benefit of the
> people standing here, that they may believe that you
> sent me."
>
> When he had said this, Jesus called in a loud voice, "Laza-
> rus, come out!" The dead man came out, his hands and
> feet wrapped with strips of linen, and a cloth around
> his face.
>
> Jesus said to them, "Take off the grave clothes and let
> him go" (verses 41-44).

This was the power of the gospel on full display. Jesus has the
power to raise the dead. Martha and Mary never conceived of such
a thing. To them, bringing Lazarus back to life was impossible. Only
those who are alive are within the realm of miracles.

Jesus could have healed Lazarus. He could have done so long-
distance by simply speaking a word. But Jesus had something else in
mind. And he wants you to have something else in mind.

God doesn't want better people. He wants new people—people
who are fully alive in him.

Are you still looking to God to improve your current situation, to make your life better? Do you still think of Christianity as a self-improvement program? Today, will you change your mind? Will you repent and believe?

Are you willing to place all that you are in the hands of Jesus, the one who is the resurrection and the life?

3

The Essence of Faith

My dad loved basketball—specifically, Kentucky basketball. Some of my fondest memories growing up were with him either watching the Wildcats play or listening to the legendary Cawood Ledford's call on the radio.

Basketball was in my dad's blood. He coached youth basketball, which means he coached me. There wasn't much he didn't know about the sport. He was involved in basketball in other ways as well. Dad was most proud of his association with the prestigious Atlanta Tipoff Club and served this organization for many years as treasurer.

At first, I didn't pay much attention to the fact that he belonged to such a prominent club. As a matter of fact, I didn't know it was so prestigious until he told me about the banquet he attended to give their award to the college player of the year. My dad was right there on the platform when they handed the trophy to Ralph Sampson of the University of Virginia. That got my attention.

The award is named after James Naismith. If you know anything about basketball, you know he invented the game. In 1891, as a teacher at the YMCA International Training College in Springfield, Massachusetts, Naismith was given the task of inventing a game students could play indoors. He had 14 days to complete the assignment.

He drew from his love of sports and his agricultural background, and an idea started to take shape in his mind. Two weeks later, Naismith delivered the game of basketball to the college administration. Thirteen basic rules spelled out how the game was to be played. Two teams competed, and the object was to get a round ball into a peach basket. The team that scored the most baskets won the game.

The game was a big hit with the college students and quickly spread to other colleges. Naismith was surprised by the game's popularity. Seven years after inventing the game, he moved to Lawrence, Kansas, to teach at the University of Kansas and to coach the basketball team. By the turn of the century, colleges began competing with each other.

Today, the game is played worldwide. Naismith has been memorialized in the basketball hall of fame and through the award that bears his name. He is known as the father of basketball. And now you know the genesis of basketball.

As it turns out, every great game, invention, or field of study has a similar beginning. Someone gets the ball rolling (so to speak), and that someone stands as the father of that particular endeavor. Hippocrates is the father of modern medicine. Adam Smith is the father of modern economics. Philo T. Farnsworth is the father of television.

The same is true for the story of faith. The story starts with Abraham. Yes, there were others, such as Abel, Enoch, and Noah, who preceded Abraham and were commended for their faith. Yet Abraham is the one who provides us with the essence of faith. He is the one Paul describes as "the father of all who believe" (Romans 4:11).

The Bible tells us we are saved by grace through faith, so it's important to take a look at the father of faith. The seminal chapters of his story are Genesis 12, 15, and 22.

The Promise

We first meet Abram (God later changed his name to Abraham) in Genesis 11. He was born in Ur of the Chaldeans. His father was Terah, and his wife was Sarai (later named Sarah). The text notes that she was barren.

Terah, the patriarch, set out with Abram, Sarai, and his grandson Lot toward Canaan. They stopped in Harran and settled there. In Harran, God spoke to Abram: "Go from your country, your people and your father's household to the land I will show you" (Genesis 12:1). Then the Lord promised Abram...

- to make him a great nation and to bless him
- to make his name great and to make him a blessing
- to bless those who blessed him and to curse those who cursed him
- to bless all peoples of the earth through him

The way Moses pens the story is intriguing to me. God spoke, here is what he said, and that's it. Look again at God's promises. These four points carry some weight. The first one alone is mind-boggling. I wonder if God's words fully registered with Abram. How did he respond? Did he ask God any questions, like how or when? Moses left all those details out of the narrative. The text simply says, "So Abram went, as the LORD had told him" (verse 4). When he arrived in Canaan with Sarai and Lot, the Lord appeared to him and said, "To your offspring I will give this land" (verse 7).

As we look back on this story through the lens of the cross and the resurrection, we see the fulfillment of all these promises in Jesus Christ. Abram did not have that vantage point, however. All he knew was that God had a plan, that God would carry it out through him somehow, and that it included the blessing of all peoples and a promised land.

Let's stop here for a moment to examine the key elements of the story thus far. The dominant figure is God. He is the main character, not Abram. He intentionally reaches out to Abram and inserts himself into Abram's story. He does so to make Abram a part of his story. God did not enter the scene with condemnation and wrath. God spoke promises and blessings into Abram's life. This is grace in action. This grace compelled Abram to be a willing participant.

The same is true of you. God showed up in your story. He spoke promises and blessings into your life through the person and work of Jesus Christ. That message prompted a response in you—faith, by God's grace. That response connected you to God's grand story.

This brings us to Genesis 15, where Abram's faith is fully formed. The chapter begins with another promise. "Do not be afraid, Abram. I am your shield, your very great reward."

Something was troubling Abram, however, and he expressed his concern to God. "Sovereign LORD, what can you give me since I remain childless and the one who will inherit my estate is Eliezer of Damascus?...You have given me no children; so a servant in my household will be my heir."

God responded, "This man will not be your heir, but a son who is your own flesh and blood will be your heir."

Then God took Abram outside and said, "Look up at the sky and count the stars—if indeed you can count them...So shall your offspring be."

God promised Abram a son.

"Abram believed the LORD, and he credited it to him as righteousness" (verse 6). Abram's response stands as a testament to genuine faith. God made a promise, and Abram took him at his word. The promise was a son. God's plan to bless the world would be carried out through him. Here is the gospel story, the story that caused Abram to believe the Lord.

Interestingly, God sealed his promise to Abram with a covenant. Scholars call it the Abrahamic covenant. It was from God to man, and it guaranteed both blessing and an inheritance.

God did not fail to keep his word. Peter explains, "Praise be to the God and Father of our Lord Jesus Christ! In his great mercy he has given us new birth into a living hope through the resurrection of Jesus Christ from the dead, and into an inheritance that can never perish, spoil or fade. This inheritance is kept in heaven for you" (1 Peter 1:3-4).

When you take God at his word, righteousness is credited to your account, just as it was credited to Abram's account. This is a key point in Paul's letter to the Romans. Read the way he connected Abraham's faith to yours: "The words 'it was credited to him' were written not for him alone, *but also for us*, to whom God will credit righteousness—for us who believe in him who raised Jesus our Lord from the dead" (Romans 4:23-24).

It is clear in this passage that our faith is connected to the resurrection of Jesus Christ. This makes me wonder about Abraham's faith. Since he is considered the father of faith, what exactly did he believe about God? Genesis 22 answers this question.

The Test

God delivered on his promise. At the age of 90, Sarah gave birth to their first child. Abraham, who was 100 years old at the time, named him Isaac.

"Some time later..." This is how Genesis 22 begins. No one knows how many years had passed or how old Isaac was at this point. Abraham and Isaac are about to face the most challenging test of their lives. Here is how their story goes.

> Some time later God tested Abraham. He said to him, "Abraham!"
>
> "Here I am," he replied.
>
> Then God said, "Take your son, your only son, whom you love—Isaac—and go to the region of Moriah. Sacrifice him there as a burnt offering on a mountain I will show you."

What a kick in the gut. Isaac was the son of promise, born to fulfill a glorious purpose. Think about what Abraham must have felt toward Isaac as he watched his son grow and mature.

And then, without warning, God tells Abraham to sacrifice him as a burnt offering. It doesn't make sense. Nor does Abraham's response. The account says that early the next morning, he got up, gathered all his supplies and Isaac, and set out to the region of Moriah. He was going to kill his son.

I read the story to a Bible study group several years back. Many of the men there that day had never heard the story. John was the first to share his thoughts. "Abraham was crazy. If he were alive today, he would be in a nuthouse." Tom likened the Genesis account to a news story topping the headlines at that time about a woman who had killed her children by drowning them. Asked why she did it, she said she heard a voice from heaven.

If Abraham's story happened today, he would be convicted and locked up in prison or diagnosed as insane and committed to a mental hospital. But the story didn't happen in our modern, sophisticated culture. Abraham lived almost 4000 years ago, and he was neither a criminal nor a lunatic. He was judged to be a man of God, rich in faith and steadfast in obedience. His willingness to sacrifice Isaac is a seminal event in the history of Christianity according to the writers of the New Testament.

High praise from the apostles, but why? What makes Abraham stand out?

Isaac's birth exploded Abraham's limited realm of possibilities and firmly planted his faith in the power of God. But now that faith was being stretched even further. Does God have power over death? If someone dies, can God raise him back to life?

Yes, God can make dead people alive again. That doesn't directly appear in the text of Genesis 22, but its fingerprints can be lifted from every verse. The New Testament writers clue us in. Concerning Abraham, the apostle Paul wrote, "As it is written: 'I have made you a father of many nations.' He is our father in the sight of God, in whom he believed—*the God who gives life to the dead* and calls into being things that were not" (Romans 4:17).

Is Paul telling us that Abraham believed God could give life to the dead? Did Abraham believe God could raise Isaac back to life? If so, that would explain Abraham's willingness to kill his son. What other compelling reason could be given for his seemingly criminal or insane action?

The writer of Hebrews tells the story through the lens of God raising the dead as well.

> By faith Abraham, when God tested him, offered Isaac as a sacrifice. He who had embraced the promises was about to sacrifice his one and only son, even though God had said to him, "It is through Isaac that your offspring will be reckoned." Abraham reasoned that God could

even raise the dead, and so in a manner of speaking, he
did receive Isaac back from death (Hebrews 11:17-19).

The Moment

Put yourself in Abraham's place. Could you do what God asked?
Could you thrust a knife into your son's heart? The inner turmoil
must have been sheer agony for Abraham.

But Abraham believed God. A covenant was in place that guaranteed Isaac as the one through whom God would bless the world.
This raises a question for us to consider. If God commanded Abraham to take Isaac's life, how would Abraham live out his belief that
God would fulfill his promise through Isaac? We know the end of
the story. Abraham obeyed and showed that he was willing to sacrifice Isaac. But how did he get to that point?

As I play it out in my mind, I see that somewhere along the three-
day journey, God's promise concerning Isaac inspired a profound
question in Abraham: "If I kill Isaac, what happens to God's promise to bless the world?" As Abraham thought deeply, he must have
come to this conclusion: "God brought Isaac into the world. If he
can do that, he must be able to raise him back to life."

Abraham and Isaac arrived at Mount Moriah, the place of sacrifice. The day had come. It was time for Abraham to do what God
had ordered. He built the altar with stoic resolve. Isaac watched with
bewilderment, wondering about the missing lamb.

Abraham grabbed Isaac and tied him to the altar. He raised the
knife...

My palms start to feel clammy and my stomach starts to hurt
every time I think about that moment and all that both Abraham
and Isaac were feeling. Yet when you read the story, calmness and
assurance cover the scene.

It's time. The decision is made. You are going to sacrifice your son. At that moment, the possibility of God raising the dead bursts forth in majestic splendor, and your heart cries out in victory, "Yes, I believe! God will bring him back!"

But before Abraham's hand moved, he heard God's voice.

"Abraham! Abraham!"

"Here I am," he replied.

"Do not lay a hand on the boy," he said. "Do not do anything to him. Now I know that you fear God, because you have not withheld from me your son, your only son" (verses 11-12).

Abraham looked up and saw a ram caught in the thicket. He sacrificed this ram instead of Isaac, and then he named the place The LORD Will Provide.

Centuries later, there was a Son, God's one and only, who was sacrificed. He was the Lamb of God who took away the sins of the world. God did provide. The belief that Abraham held in his heart, the belief that God gives life to the dead, took shape in power and majesty as God raised his one and only Son back to life.

Abraham knew God's awesome power and his faithfulness to deliver on his promises. He had witnessed it with the birth of Isaac. When told to take Isaac's life, he reasoned that God could raise him back to life. His faith was rewarded. The writer of Hebrews put it this way: "In a manner of speaking, he did receive Isaac back from death."

Can you imagine the joy that flooded Abraham's soul? His son was alive.

God reaffirmed his promise to Abraham that the world would be blessed through his seed because he obeyed the Lord. And it has.

Jesus came into the world. He died and rose again. Those who hear and believe that he was raised from the dead have life in his name.

Abraham listened to God, and he understood the ramifications. That's what it means to obey. He offered Isaac because he understood God's awesome power. As James wrote, "His faith and his actions were working together, and his faith was made complete by what he did" (James 2:22). Abraham believed in new life.

That's the story. Abraham's belief is the heart and soul of Christian faith. We believe God gives life to the dead. All of Christianity hinges on this reality. If Jesus was not raised, then our faith is futile and we are still in our sins. But because he was raised, we know that we too have been raised to walk in new life.

Abraham was tested. At the critical moment, his faith proved genuine. He truly believed God had power over death. God asks you to believe exactly the same truth. Ask yourself, do you believe that God has power over death?

Look at Romans 10:8-9: "[This is] the message concerning faith that we proclaim: If you declare with your mouth, 'Jesus is Lord,' and believe in your heart that God raised him from the dead, you will be saved." Notice that the cross is not mentioned. Nor is our need for forgiveness. Faith is clearly tied to resurrection.

Here is where belief in the resurrection is crucial. If you do not believe God raised Jesus from the dead, you're not going to believe he can give you a new life.

At the time, Abraham was probably the only person on the planet who believed God could give life to the dead. The guys in my Bible study group initially judged Abraham as crazy. From the world's standpoint, that's understandable—but not from God's. Abraham was so convinced of God's power to raise the dead that when God told him to sacrifice his son, he offered up Isaac. This belief in God's ability to bring life out of death defined Abraham's reality, shaped his being, and prompted radical action. And God was pleased.

It is a question that brings us right back to Abraham and Isaac. Abraham was "fully persuaded that God had power to do what he had promised" (Romans 4:21), and God credited him with righteousness. This is also true of us who believe in him who raised Jesus our Lord from the dead.

Death is not a problem to God. He has power over death. That first Easter was a glorious, earthshaking demonstration. Jesus, who was dead, was raised to life. He directs that same power toward us and makes us alive in him. This is Christianity. This is the cornerstone of our faith.

Resurrection defies human reason and logic, but so does God. He is the God who gives life to the dead.

Here are the facts. Three days after Jesus's body was laid in a borrowed tomb, God raised him from the dead. Let me ask: Do you really believe this to be true? Has it captured your heart and soul?

If not, perhaps it's time for you to step into the faith of Abraham and experience the reality of resurrection.

4

The Crossover

During my college days, I worked as a hospital orderly. It was not the most glamorous job in the world. The job description left little to be desired, but I thought it would look good on my medical school application. And besides, I met many interesting people. One of my favorites was an 87-year-old gentleman named Jim.

I was paged to his room one evening. I never liked getting paged. It usually meant being called on to perform an unpleasant task. I could share several with you, but they are far too gory for print. I didn't know what was in store for me this night. I took the elevator down and headed to Jim's room.

When I arrived, Jim's nurse filled me in on what needed to be done. The task was not so bad. While I was taking care of him, I struck up a conversation. Just small talk at first, but it quickly escalated to a serious level.

I started off by asking Jim what he had done in life. He had worked as a maître d' in one of the finer restaurants in Atlanta. He shared several stories of celebrities he had met. Then he asked about my life. I mentioned that I was a Christian. I could tell this sparked his curiosity. He started asking me what I knew about God.

His honesty was refreshing. In a matter-of-fact way, he admitted, "I've never had any real beliefs about God. I believe he exists, but it never made any difference to me."

I told him about Jesus. I told him that Jesus had died for him and was raised from the dead so that he could have eternal life. And I read several passages of Scripture to him that revealed God's love for him. He was taking in every word. I knew I was watching a miracle in the making.

After I read the last passage, I asked him if he would like to receive Jesus into his life. We prayed together. He expressed his faith in Christ with such simplicity and ease. His words were drenched with humility and thankfulness, and he spoke them directly to Jesus. In essence, he said, "Lord, I believe." He was so focused on Christ, I think I could have left the room and he would have never known. During that prayer, Jim seemed to be drawn into the arms of his heavenly Father. And he was. When he opened his eyes, Jim was a new man.

Every day following, I went to his room to talk with him and read Bible verses to him. The transformation in Jim's countenance and outlook was incredible. Life had entered his being. God had brought his dead spirit to life.

His enthusiasm was contagious. "I'm going to shout this message from the rooftop," he told me one day. "If I ever get out of this hospital, I'm going to proclaim it to the world."

Jim didn't make it out of the hospital. However, in the three weeks after coming to know Christ, he shouted the message from his hospital bed. Every nurse, every doctor, every staff member who cared for him heard him proclaim the resurrection of Christ Jesus.

What happened to Jim? I describe it as the crossover. Through faith in Jesus Christ, he crossed over from death to life, just as Jesus said people would. "Very truly I tell you, whoever hears my word and believes him who sent me has eternal life and will not be judged but has crossed over from death to life" (John 5:24). This is what happened to Jim. This is what happens to anyone who trusts in Jesus.

One afternoon while carrying out my duties on the orthopedic floor, I heard, "Code blue, room 325" over the intercom. This was Jim's room. I took off running, but in the depths of my soul I knew my friend was now with the Lord. When I got there, the doctors had already pronounced him dead. But I knew the truth. Jim was fully alive and in the presence of the Lord.

The trajectory of my life changed that day. I had wanted to be a physician. I wanted to help sick people get well. At least that was the line I used when describing my goals and dreams. In reality, I wanted all the things that come with being a physician—the money, the prestige, and the respect. When I learned about the grace of God in that Atlanta Bible study, the idea of being a physician started to lose its appeal. That pursuit for money, prestige, and respect seemed empty.

Watching Jim come to life in Christ put a new dream and a new passion in me. I wanted to be a part of God's great rescue mission in some way. I wanted to connect people to Christ's resurrection story and see others cross over from death to life.

The Wrong Place

The grass is always greener on the other side. This cliché speaks to our longing for something better. We get dissatisfied with where we are and start to look elsewhere. Sadly, when we do journey to the other side, we often find the grass isn't as green as we thought it would be. The point is to find contentment right now, right where we are.

However, on a spiritual level, the cliché carries some truth. Before we trusted Christ and were made alive in him, we were not where we were supposed to be. We were in the wrong place.

We can blame this on Adam and Eve. They were in the right place and enjoying genuine contentment. You remember the story. After God created Adam and Eve, he placed them in the Garden of Eden. That's where they belonged. That's where they could fulfill their greatest purpose.

But all that changed when the crafty serpent entered the picture. Adam and Eve gave in to his cunning scheme. They ate of the tree of the knowledge of good and evil. They chose to be independent from God, and in so doing they forfeited his life. They died spiritually. No longer were they welcome in the Garden.

In an act of mercy and grace, the Lord clothed Adam and Eve with animal skins and expelled them from the Garden.

> The LORD God banished him from the Garden of Eden to work the ground from which he had been taken. After he drove the man out, he placed on the east side of the Garden of Eden cherubim and a flaming sword flashing back and forth to guard the way to the tree of life (Genesis 3:23-24).

They were now in the wrong place. They were not where they were supposed to be.

Their sin landed all of us in the wrong place. That place is called darkness. It is a horrible place to be. It's where sin and death rule.

Have you ever felt as if you weren't where you were supposed to be in life? I think we all feel this way at one time or another. When we were lost, that feeling was based on truth. We weren't in the right place at all.

Jesus entered into our world of darkness as the light of life. His own did not receive him as Messiah. Even after seeing his many miracles, they still refused to believe. But to those who did believe, he gave this promise: "I have come into the world as a light, so that no one who believes in me should stay in darkness" (John 12:46).

Think about this. You were in the dark. It was the wrong place to be. Then Jesus entered in and said, "I am the light of the world. Whoever follows me will never walk in darkness, but will have the light of life" (John 8:12). You were rescued. Jesus grabbed you out of the darkness and placed you into his wonderful light (1 Peter 2:9). Paul explained it this way: "He has rescued us from the dominion of darkness and brought us into the kingdom of the Son he loves" (Colossians 1:13).

To cross over from death to life is to cross from darkness to light.

The Wrong Person

We were not only in the wrong place but also under the control of the wrong person. Adam and Eve only *thought* they were choosing independence. What they really chose was bondage. That tree of the knowledge of good and evil had never caught Adam's and Eve's eyes before Satan came along. Only then did this tree look desirable. Only then did they want to be like God. Only then were they willing to "exchange the truth about God for a lie" (Romans 1:25).

Darkness is ruled by dark forces. Contrary to what we think, no one is independent or free. Everyone is under the control of someone else.

When you lived in the dark, "You followed the ways of this world and of the ruler of the kingdom of the air, the spirit who is now at work in those who are disobedient" (Ephesians 2:2). John put it this way: "The one who does what is sinful is of the devil, because the devil has been sinning from the beginning" (1 John 3:8). This is a tough truth to swallow. It smacks our pride and ego. We want to stand up and shout, "Don't tell me someone else is calling the shots. I'm living life my way!"

That's exactly what Satan wants us to think. He is so clever and deceitful. He made Adam and Eve think the idea to eat of the tree of the knowledge of good and evil was their own. The "ruler of the kingdom of the air" does the same to us. But in reality, the choices we made in the darkness were laid out for us by the world system. We were merely following the ways of the world.

The world offers only a few things on its menu. These items have been preselected for you. Read the fine print—"No substitutions." The offerings may be presented to you in different ways, but the choices the world offers boils down to these three: "For everything in the world—the lust of the flesh, the lust of the eyes, and the pride of life—comes not from the Father but from the world" (1 John 2:16).

When Jesus rescued you, he set you free from the world system. He released you from its power. He turned you "from darkness to light, and from the power of Satan to God" (Acts 26:18).

To cross over from death to life is to cross from bondage to freedom.

The Wrong Purpose

One of the big three questions we ask is, "Why am I here?" This is a question about purpose. In the realm of darkness, purpose is where we miss the mark. We don't carry out God's desires for us.

Instead, we live for ourselves. This starts early in life. If you are a parent, you know this is true. Kids are naturally selfish. They don't like to share. They believe the world revolves around them. Jeanna and I have pointed that out to our kids many times.

The Bible says that "all of us lived among them at one time, gratifying the cravings of our flesh and following its desires and thoughts. Like the rest, we were by nature deserving of wrath" (Ephesians 2:3). That's missing the mark. God didn't create us for this purpose. He had something else in mind.

I wrestled with this question for many years. Other people seemed to know their purpose in life. They had a plan and a direction. I felt stuck in the mud. Nothing seemed that important to me. Solomon must have felt the same way when he wrote, "Everything is meaningless." Discovering the grace of God cut through my confusion and helped me see that God did have a purpose for me. I was on this earth for a reason. Whew!

Paul encouraged the Philippians, "Continue to work out your salvation with fear and trembling, for it is God who works in you to will and to act in order to fulfill his good purpose" (Philippians 2:12-13). God works in us every minute of every day so we will choose and act according to his good purpose. It's a process that aligns our hearts and minds with his. Your purpose is this: to work out in day-to-day life what God is working in you.

It can look different every day. That's what makes the Christian life the most exciting adventure of all. The day I met Jim, God had a purpose in mind—to help someone who was dead in sin cross over to life in Christ. God had been working a desire in my heart to share the gospel with others. With Jim, that desire was worked out. I had never been a part of something as exciting as that. God let me participate in his work. Talk about meaning and purpose in life!

When you received Jesus, you received a new purpose. I think

Peter struggled with his purpose in life, especially after he denied the Lord. Jesus restored him by saying, "Feed my sheep." Peter got the message. He helped many others find their purpose in life. He addressed this issue in his first letter: "As a result, they do not live the rest of their earthly lives for evil human desires, but rather for the will of God. For you have spent enough time in the past doing what pagans choose to do—living in debauchery, lust, drunkenness, orgies, carousing and detestable idolatry" (1 Peter 4:2-3).

To cross over from death to life is to cross over to a new purpose in life.

The Wrong Identity

There is something else that Adam handed down to us—the wrong identity. Through his disobedience, we "were made sinners" (Romans 5:19). God did not create us as sinners. Yet that is what we became in Adam. This truth is hard for us to admit. Face it—we have a hard time admitting we've sinned. We sanitize our choices to make them seem not so bad. "I messed up," we say. Or "I made a mistake." Rarely do we say, "I sinned."

When you were a citizen of darkness, you were a sinner.

While Jesus was on earth, he gravitated toward sinners. This confounded the religious leaders. They wondered why he hung out with the dregs of society. They didn't understand his mission. Paul was one of those religious leaders. But when Paul looked intently into the mirror of the law, he saw the truth. He ripped off his mask and his self-righteous garments and boldly proclaimed, "I am the chief of sinners."

As he wrote, "Here is a trustworthy saying that deserves full acceptance: Christ Jesus came into the world to save sinners" (1 Timothy 1:15). Jesus hung out with sinners because they were his mission. There is nothing to fear in admitting the truth. As I shared in the introduction, "while we were still sinners, Christ died for us" (Romans 5:8).

Jesus saves sinners, and every time he does, he gives each one a new identity. The day you were saved, you got a brand-new identity. It happened through new birth. You were born into Adam's family as a sinner. You were born again into Jesus's family as a child of God. "To all who did receive him," John wrote, "to those who believed in his name, he gave the right to become children of God—children born not of natural descent, nor of human decision or a husband's will, but born of God" (John 1:12-13).

By grace through faith, you became a child of God. You could never work your way up to this status. It is unattainable through human effort. You arrived there because God made you alive in Christ. As a result, you can echo John's words:

> See what great love the Father has lavished on us, that we should be called children of God! And that is what we are! The reason the world does not know us is that it did not know him. Dear friends, now we are children of God, and what we will be has not yet been made known. But we know that when Christ appears, we shall be like him, for we shall see him as he is. All who have this hope in him purify themselves, just as he is pure (1 John 3:1-3).

Crossing over from death to life means crossing over to a brand-new identity.

The Bridge

Jesus Christ bridges the gap between death and life. We cross over through him. There is no other way. I know that sounds exclusive and politically incorrect. But it is also the most loving thing you or I can say.

Life is found in Jesus Christ—nowhere else. This is the testimony of God the Father concerning his Son: "God has given us eternal life, and this life is in his Son. Whoever has the Son has life; whoever does not have the Son of God does not have life" (1 John 5:11-12). It's that simple and that clear.

This is another sticking point for many people. They claim there is more than one way to God. But it misses the point. Our need is life. Jesus Christ is the only person who can give us life. As Paul noted in his defense of the resurrection, Jesus is "a life-giving spirit" (1 Corinthians 15:45).

If you are struggling with this idea, maybe this illustration will help. Cancer is a horrible disease. Research teams all over the world are feverishly working to find a cure. Let's say that a research team in Chicago discovers the cure. They develop a drug and have exclusive rights to administer it to any person willing to travel to their facilities.

What would you tell someone who had cancer? "If you want to be cured, go to Chicago."

"Well, what about all those fine research teams in Atlanta, London, and Hong Kong?"

"They may be doing fine work, but they don't have the cure for cancer. There is only one place you can go, and that is to the cancer research facility in Chicago. Those who go get cured. Those who don't go there don't get cured."

Jesus couldn't have said it any clearer. "I am the way and the truth and the life. No one comes to the Father except through me" (John 14:6). He is the way out of death into life. He is the way out of darkness into light. He is the cure the world needs.

My friend Jim crossed over from death to life through Jesus Christ. Here is the good news. If you have confessed with your mouth that Jesus is Lord and have believed in your heart that God raised him from the dead, you too have crossed over from death to life. You have received the cure.

That's news worth shouting from the rooftops.

Great Expectations

In 1980, a freshman sensation by the name of Herschel Walker turned the Georgia Bulldog nation upside down. He hailed from a small town in South Georgia. During his senior year in high school, he was the most recruited football player in the nation. He could go to any school he wanted. Thankfully, he chose Georgia.

I was a UGA senior that year.

Herschel's first game was against Tennessee at Neyland Stadium before 105,000 screaming, orange-clad Volunteer fans. It was late in the game before Vince Dooley, the head coach, sent Walker in at the tailback position. Dooley was an old-school coach—freshmen did not start.

Everybody in the stands and watching on TV knew the kid was going to get the ball. On his first carry as a college player, he broke through the line into an open field. Bill Bates, the Tennessee safety, was the only defender standing between Herschel and the goal line. Herschel lowered his head, bowled Bates over, and pranced into the end zone. Larry Munson, the Bulldog announcer and the biggest homer in college sports, let loose, "Oh my God, oh my God—and this kid is just a freshman!"

At the first home game, the chants began. From the north stands, 40,000 fans yelled, "Herschel." The 40,000 fans in the south stands responded, "Walker." This continued all game long. I can almost hear the chants now: "Herschel!" "Walker!" "Herschel!" "Walker!" Oh my, was he fun to watch.

He was a man among boys. There was no limit to what he could accomplish on the field. Okay, I admit, I'm a big Herschel fan. In my mind, he was and is the greatest college football player to have ever played the game. I was there. I saw him. I've never seen anyone better. Every time he touched the ball, the crowd roared to its feet, anticipating another incredible touchdown run. He was quick and fast and strong and determined. He wanted to win.

The team finished the season 11–0. No one expected that when the season started. About halfway through the season, expectations changed. The fans and sports gurus started to talk about Georgia as the favorite to win the national championship. Expectations reached that level because an 18-year-old kid showed up on the scene. He was that good.

Georgia played Notre Dame for the national championship at the Sugar Bowl in New Orleans. For four days, the town was a sea of red and black. This was Georgia's time to shine. My ticket for the game was in the top row of the Superdome. It didn't matter. I was in the house to witness the most exciting moment in Bulldog history.

Herschel dislocated his collarbone early in the game. This sent a scare through the Georgia fan base. But injury or not, Walker was not coming out of the game. Dooley continued to call his number.

He continued to perform. The game was on Herschel's shoulders. That's exactly where he wanted it to be.

The two teams fought hard, and the competition was fierce. In the end, Herschel's warrior spirit willed the Bulldogs to a 17–10 victory. As the clock ticked down to zero, Georgia had their first national championship. Bulldog Nation was number one in the land.

Herschel Walker single-handedly raised the expectations of the Georgia football program. He played for three years. Those three years were characterized by great expectations. With him on the team, the Bulldogs expected to play for the national championship every year. And they did. Herschel's presence turned great expectations into reality.

I think about that national championship run often. Those are the glory days for UGA. We are waiting for the next Herschel to show up and return the Bulldogs to their glory.

When I think about this story, I think about the great expectations we can and should have as believers. The good news is that someone showed up. Jesus is on the scene. When you put your full weight of trust in the gospel, you get him. And with him, everything changes.

Here's What Happened

For a few years, Jeanna and I were *American Idol* fans. Each season, the producers of the show set up auditions in key cities around the country. These auditions draw thousands and thousands of people with dreams of making it big. One by one, they showcase their talents before a panel of judges. The judges listen and decide right then and there to send the contestant to Hollywood or back home. If the judges say yes, the contestant is given a golden ticket, which serves as his entry into the next round.

Sadly, many see salvation as nothing more than a golden ticket that will grant them entry into heaven when they die. Yes, we are immediately present with the Lord when we die. That's our hope. However, don't limit salvation to a guarantee of heaven. That's only part of the story. As we discussed in chapter 2, salvation is God's act of grace to make us spiritually alive. Through faith in Jesus Christ, we cross over from death to life. And something else happens as well.

The good news is also about God finding a home in us. This is a story line that runs through the Bible. Think about the tabernacle Moses built and the temple Solomon built. When they were conse-crated, God filled them with his presence, as evidenced by fire and smoke. These were striking and powerful images, but they were shadows of God's real plan. As Paul said to the philosophers on Mars Hill, "God...does not live in temples built by human hands" (Acts 17:24). He had another location in mind—within his people. This is the story of Pentecost.

Luke tells the story in Acts 2. It takes place in Jerusalem during the annual celebration of Pentecost. Jews from every nation were gathered. The disciples were together in a house, waiting, just as Jesus told them to. "Wait for the gift my Father promised...John baptized with water, but in a few days you will be baptized with the Holy Spirit" (Acts 1:4-5).

When the day of Pentecost arrived, something strange happened. A loud sound like "the blowing of a violent wind" filled the house, and tongues of fire rested on each of the disciples. They began to speak about the glories of God, and everyone heard the message in their native language. Naturally, folks began to ask, "What does this mean?"

Peter stood to explain. What occurred that day was prophesied by Joel. God was pouring out his Spirit on humanity. A new temple was being dedicated. God was filling it with his presence.

Your personal Pentecost occurred the day you received Jesus Christ. At that moment, God filled your life with his presence. Salvation is Christ coming to live in you—"Christ in you, the hope of glory" (Colossians 1:27).

Apparently, this truth was not readily understood. Paul asked the Corinthian church, "Don't you know that you yourselves are God's temple and that God's Spirit dwells in your midst?" (1 Corinthians 3:16).

We shouldn't overlook this truth. Don't move through this section too quickly. Take time and think through the ramifications. His presence in our lives changes everything. The God of the universe is living in you. His love, grace, truth, and power are now coursing through your spiritual veins.

Now all your hopes and expectations for life are pinned to him. Jesus showed up. He is on the scene. As a result, you can live with great expectations. Let's take a look at three things you can expect simply because Jesus Christ is alive and living in you.

Assurance of Salvation

Many verses in the Bible make the case for eternal security. The strongest come from the mouth of Jesus. Here is what he said about those who hear his voice and follow him:

> I give them eternal life, and they shall never perish; no one will snatch them out of my hand. My Father, who has given them to me, is greater than all; no one is able to snatch them out of the Father's hand. I and the Father are one (John 10:28-30).

This is what Jesus said. These are red-letter words. This statement alone should settle any argument over our assurance of salvation. He gives us eternal life, and as a result, we will never perish. We are in his hands. Who can snatch us out? The apostle John makes the same case in his first letter.

> And this is the testimony: God has given us eternal life, and this life is in his Son. Whoever has the Son has life; whoever does not have the Son of God does not have life.
>
> I write these things to you who believe in the name of the Son of God that you may know that you have eternal life (1 John 5:11-13).

You can know you have eternal life. According to John, this isn't a matter for debate. If you have the Son, you have eternal life. Do you have the Son? Then what do you have?

These are powerful passages. If you haven't memorized them, I encourage you to do so. But here is the deal. Your memory can let you down or get drowned out by the many opposing voices in the world. And as if that weren't enough, the accuser comes along to stir up any shred of doubt he can find. He does everything in his power to keep you from walking in the assurance you have in Christ.

God knows all about Satan. He knows his schemes and plans. That's one reason God sent his Spirit to live inside you. Your memory may fail you, but God's Spirit never will. Read what Paul wrote concerning the work of God's Spirit in your life:

> The Spirit you received does not make you slaves, so that you live in fear again; rather, the Spirit you received brought about your adoption to sonship. And by him we cry, "*Abba*, Father." The Spirit himself testifies with our spirit that we are God's children (Romans 8:15-16).

Are you getting the idea that God wants you to know you are saved? It is so important to him that he asked the Spirit to make this truth real in your heart. Your assurance is on the Spirit's shoulders. He is up to the task.

One of the most asked questions on the *Basic Gospel* radio broadcast is this: "How can I know I'm saved?" If you want to know where the majority of Christians struggle, it is with this issue. Let's face it. We don't always act perfect, and our thoughts aren't always pure and noble. Take a look at all the things you've thought, said, and done just today. That will give you plenty of reasons to doubt your salvation. So what do you do with those doubts?

Paul issued this challenge to the Corinthians: "Examine yourselves to see whether you are in the faith; test yourselves. Do you not realize that Christ Jesus is in you—unless, of course, you fail the test?" (2 Corinthians 13:5).

If Jesus Christ is in you, you've passed the test. His Spirit is testifying with your spirit right now that you are a child of God. That testimony is in your heart.

If you feel like you failed the test, that's okay. God is using your doubts and fears and those nagging questions to draw you to himself. Don't go another second without receiving him. As I tell people, drive the stake. Let today, this very moment, be the day of salvation for you. God is showing up right now in your situation to make you alive together with Christ. I encourage you to receive him by faith.

Several years ago, I taught a conference in Colorado. One day for lunch, I joined a couple attending from Dallas. After I sat down, I noticed that Bonnie had a huge smile on her face. I said to her, "You sure look happy today." She was.

She proceeded to tell me her story. "Bob, today I got it. For the first time, the gospel made sense to me, and I know I'm saved." That night in her room, she penned a letter. Several weeks later she gave me a copy.

June 6, 2010, is the first day of my new life…I think I had received Jesus as my Savior, but I was not 100 percent sure. Today, now, I know I have. I am accepted…I am a forgiven child of God…I am righteous before the one great God. He is my Father. Jesus Christ is my Savior and friend for eternity.

With Christ living in you, you can walk in assurance.

Say No to Sin

Yes, I am saying that you can expect to say no to sin as a believer in Christ.

Many try and many fail, but they go about it the wrong way. They rely on willpower and sheer grit to withstand the onslaught. Believe me—that strategy will never work. Take up the fight against sin on your own, and you will lose every time.

Your ability to say no is the result of the Holy Spirit's work in your life. His work on this front never ends. This is grace in action, teaching us to say no to "ungodliness and worldly passions, and to live self-controlled, upright and godly lives in this present age" (Titus 2:11). He consistently teaches us this powerful lesson. The lesson is built on one foundational truth—"You, dear children, are from God and have overcome them, because the one who is in you is greater than the one who is in the world" (1 John 4:4).

You have Christ living in you. He has already proven through his resurrection that sin and death are no match for him. He won the battle. Now his victory is your victory.

This sounds nice, but how does it work practically?

This is where faith comes into play. In his letter to the Galatians, Paul likens faith to a walk: "So I say, walk by the Spirit, and you will not gratify the desires of the flesh" (Galatians 5:16). What he means by this is that we are to order our lives around the Holy Spirit. In other words, follow his lead. Keep in step with what he is doing in your life.

This is where you will find the real excitement in life. It's not out there in the world. It's in Jesus.

So what is the Holy Spirit doing in your life right now? Maybe he is putting a desire in your heart to forgive someone who hurt you. If so, step out in faith and forgive. Keeping in step with the Spirit in this situation means you will not carry out the desire of your flesh to get even or seek revenge. Maybe he is working on your tongue so you will use it to speak honestly and to build others up instead of tearing them down. If so, step out in faith—tell the truth and encourage others with your words. When you do, you will not carry out the desire of your flesh to tear others down.

Saying yes to God's Spirit means you will not carry out the desires of the flesh.

With Christ in you, you can say no to sin.

Bear Fruit

Not long after I graduated from college, a fraternity brother committed suicide. The news was shocking—and devastating. No one saw it coming. He was so positive and energetic. He had also made it big in the oil industry. His suicide didn't make sense.

I learned later that he had leveraged his assets too far. When the oil industry tanked, his financial empire crumbled beneath him. While this was happening, he maintained the appearance that everything was just fine even though turmoil raged in his soul. What he wanted was peace, but it never came. In his darkest hour, he chose to take his life. I can only speculate, but I believe he felt this was the only way for him to find peace.

Through the years, I've taught many small group Bible studies for men. When I've asked them what they want most in life, the number one answer is peace. The pressures of life can do all sorts of things inside us. Fear and anger can fill our minds, and restlessness can disturb our souls. We get to the point where all we want is a little peace. Many men have asked me, "What do I need to do to have peace in my life?"

It's not out there in the world. And you can't buy it. Peace comes from God. It is the fruit of his Spirit, along with love, joy, patience, kindness, goodness, faithfulness, gentleness, and self-control (Galatians 5:22-23).

Jesus provided a wonderful illustration to show us how to bear this fruit. The illustration is the vine and the branch. He taught it this way: "I am the vine; you are the branches. If you remain in me and I in you, you will bear much fruit; apart from me you can do nothing" (John 15:5).

As the vine, Jesus is the source of all the things we desperately seek in life. Where does Jesus live? In us. In you.

Again, the point is that everything you need is found in Jesus Christ. And he is living in you. Abide in him. Remain in him. Live in him, and you will bear fruit. This is just another way of saying, walk in the Spirit.

It seems simple, doesn't it? It is, because the real work is God's. We simply bear the fruit of his work in us. It is by grace through faith.

With Christ in you, you will bear the fruit of his Spirit.

Are you a believer? Have you placed your full weight of trust in the one who died and rose again? If so, Jesus Christ has found a home in your heart. Expect him to do great things in and through you.

Part 2

Forgiveness

God is the God who forgives.
MIROSLAV VOLF, *FREE OF CHARGE*

6

It Is Finished!

On the *Basic Gospel* radio broadcast, we talk about all kinds of life issues, but none more than forgiveness of sins. Year in and year out, forgiveness ranks as the number one issue our listeners are most concerned about.

I understand why. As the Bible declares, "all have sinned and fall short of the glory of God" (Romans 3:23). We prove this verse every day we live. Each time we sin, questions about forgiveness race through our minds. Many times, we ignore the questions, the guilt, and the fear. We bury them all inside and hope tomorrow will be a better day. Eventually, however, the questions and the guilt and the fear demand our attention. That was the case for my friend Chris.

He was 95 percent sure he was okay with God. For a long time, this was just fine with him. He knew the day he trusted Christ for salvation and knew he was a Christian. At least he was 95 percent sure.

Sin has a way of rocking the boat. It did in Chris's life. There was a particular sin he could not shake. Maybe that's the case for you. It was in my life. My prayers were like a broken record. "Lord, I did it again. Please forgive me, and I promise I will do better tomorrow." This was Chris's story as well. He prayed. He read his Bible. He went to church. He promised God he would do better and try harder. But nothing worked.

Doubts that were once dormant were now fully awake. Sin issued the wakeup call. Chris's 5 percent of uncertainty was now occupying 100 percent of his thinking. The security and assurance he once knew gave way to fear and anxiety. Many nights he tossed and turned, wondering whether his sins had been forgiven. And if not, could they be forgiven? Ignoring the issue was no longer an option.

Desperate for answers, Chris picked up the phone and called our national radio broadcast. With thousands of people listening in, he shared his story and then asked, "Will God forgive me for what I've done?"

Chris's story is not unique. His doubts and fears are shared by Christians everywhere. We know Christ died on our behalf, but we are not sure what this means to us on a personal level. As a result, we live in fear of God's punishment. This was my story, and it's the story of many of our listeners who call our ministry seeking help.

Based on 30-plus years of ministry experience, I've come to these observations.

- All Christians know that Christ died to forgive their sins.
- Even with the clear declaration of God's Word that our sins—past, present, and future—have been forgiven through the finished work of Jesus Christ, Christians

still struggle with fear and guilt. They wonder whether they've been forgiven.

- Confusion on this most fundamental truth hampers every other aspect of the Christian life.

Please let these observations sink in—particularly the third one. The first issue I address with someone struggling to live the Christian life is the forgiveness of their sins. Most often, that is where the problem lies. A life filled with confusion and doubts and fears is not what God wants for you. He wants to clear away these things in your life, and he does so by connecting you to his great love for you.

It's at the cross we see this love in action. As Jesus explained, "Greater love has no one than this: to lay down one's life for one's friends" (John 15:13). As Miroslav Volf, a theology professor at Yale, wrote in his book *Free of Charge*, "God is the God who forgives." Jesus's act of grace through death brings this forgiveness to our hearts.

Let me ask you. Do you know that God has forgiven your sins? If not, do you long to know God's forgiveness? Do you want to experience rest and peace and assurance?

The gospel proclaims that you can know and experience God's forgiveness. What you are looking for is found in Christ's finished work on the cross. That's where we led Chris to help him settle the forgiveness issue once and for all.

If you want to grow in your relationship with Jesus Christ and experience his love, the cross is the place to start. That all-important question, "Will God forgive my sin?" is answered in the death of Jesus Christ.

In the first part of the book, we learned about the new life we have in Jesus Christ. His first priority for you is to take you from spiritual death to spiritual life. The good news is that by grace you were made alive together with him. You have the life of Jesus Christ in you. Forgiveness frees you to live that new life to the full.

Why the Cross?

At a breakthrough moment for the disciples and a turning point in Jesus's ministry, "Jesus began to explain to his disciples that he must go to Jerusalem and suffer many things at the hands of the elders, chief priests and teachers of the law, and that he must be killed and on the third day be raised to life" (Matthew 16:21). The Gospels include seven instances of Jesus emphasizing this.

Through his teachings and miracles, Jesus had caused quite a stir among the people of Israel. The watercooler talk had people wondering who this miracle worker was. Jesus took his disciples aside and asked them, "Who do people say that I am?" Then he turned the question on them. "Who do you say that I am?" (verses 13,15). This is the most compelling and most important question that has ever been asked.

What about you? Who do you say that Jesus is? If he is simply a good man, a great teacher, or even a prophet, that raises all sorts of questions about the validity of his sacrifice on the cross. How could the death of a mere man take away your sins? His identity as both Lord and God validates everything he said or did. When he says to you, "Your sins are forgiven," you can rest assured that they are.

After Jesus asked the question, Peter stood to answer. With confidence in his voice, he declared, "You are the Messiah, the Son of the living God" (verse 16). This wasn't information Peter figured out on his own. God the Father revealed the truth to him. Jesus gave high praise to Peter and even promised to give him the keys of the kingdom of heaven. A "wow" moment for the disciples.

But then, suddenly, Jesus turned the conversation to his impending death. Peter was dumbfounded. He took Jesus aside and rebuked him.

What was Peter thinking? Who in their right mind rebukes the Son of the living God? Peter, that's who. "Never, Lord!" he said. "This shall never happen to you!" (verse 22).

This brought a swift response from the Lord. "Get behind me, Satan!" (verse 23). Peter's shining moment was tarnished in a flash.

Peter didn't understand why Jesus had to die. It made no sense to him. The other disciples were just as confused. Why did Jesus have to die? It was a puzzling question. Sometimes it is for us as well. We need the right perspective. We need to "have in mind the concerns of God," not "merely human concerns" (verse 23). Jesus's death was part of God's plan. Without it there is no forgiveness of sins. The writer of Hebrews stated this truth clearly: "Without the shedding of blood there is no forgiveness" (Hebrews 9:22).

Hebrews 9:22 is a foundational verse. It answers the why of the cross. Everything about forgiveness is built on top of it. If you haven't done so, mark this verse in your Bible. When you struggle, remember, Christ shed his blood for you. That means there is forgiveness of sins. And in Christ, you already have it. The death of Jesus Christ is the way of forgiveness.

What can we take from this? First, God desires to forgive. He doesn't want you to face the judgment and the penalty your sins deserve. Second, Christ was willing to carry out the desire of his Father. Consider these words: "Then I said, 'Here I am—it is written about me in the scroll—I have come to do your will, my God'" (Hebrews 10:7). Jesus died to do the will of his Father. His death delivered forgiveness to you. There was no other way.

His Final Steps

Jesus's final week began with his triumphant march into Jerusalem. The people laid palm branches at his feet and hailed him as their King. Their hallelujahs were short-lived, however. Later that week, Judas betrayed Jesus to the religious leaders, who arrested him in the Garden of Gethsemane. The high priest and elders interrogated Jesus, mocked him, and beat him through the night, hoping to find evidence to condemn him to death. In their madness, these priests and elders searched high and low for anyone who would come forward to testify. Two finally did, but their stories were rife with holes.

Determined to find something, Caiaphas, the high priest at the time, pressed Jesus. "Tell us if you are the Messiah, the Son of God."

"You have said so," Jesus answered.

At this, Caiaphas tore his clothes. "He has spoken blasphemy!" he cried. "Why do we need any more witnesses?"

The chief priests and the whole Sanhedrin condemned him to die. Early the next morning, they took Jesus to Pilate, the Roman governor.

Pilate questioned him intensely and found him innocent. He then sent Jesus to be questioned by Herod, the tetrarch over the region of Galilee. Herod had heard many stories about Jesus. He gladly met with Jesus and hoped to see a miracle. But Herod's questions and requests went unanswered, so he sent Jesus back to Pilate.

Pilate wanted nothing to do with him. He hoped to release him by using one of the Jewish customs. Pilate brought out Jesus and Barabbas, a murderer and thief. He asked, "Do you want me to release to you the King of the Jews?" Stirred by the Jewish leaders, the crowd called for the release of Barabbas.

Shocked, Pilate asked, "What shall I do, then, with Jesus who is called the Messiah?"

"Crucify him!" the crowd shouted.

In a cowardly act, Pilate gave in to their demands. He had Jesus flogged and then handed him over to be crucified.

Calvary

Jesus was crucified between two criminals at a place called the Skull, or Golgotha. We call it Calvary. It was nine in the morning when the soldiers nailed his hands and feet to the cross and then suspended him between heaven and earth.

The soldiers gambled for his clothes.

Passersby jeered him.

The chief priest and elders mocked him.

The criminal to his left scorned him.

The one to his right pleaded for mercy.

At noon the sky darkened. It was the darkest moment in human history. God was making Jesus, the one who had no sin, to be sin for us (2 Corinthians 5:21).

At three in the afternoon, Jesus said in a loud voice, "My God, my God, why have you forsaken me?"

And then in victory, he cried out, "It is finished!"

With that, he gave up his spirit. Many strange things happened at that moment.

> The curtain of the temple was torn in two from top to bottom. The earth shook, the rocks split and the tombs broke open. The bodies of many holy people who had died were raised to life. They came out of the tombs after Jesus' resurrection and went into the holy city and appeared to many people (Matthew 27:51-53).

This was no ordinary death, and it was suffered by no ordinary person. This was Jesus, the Lord and Creator of all, offering himself as the perfect Lamb of God. His achievement removed the barrier that stood between God and man. It shook the foundation of the world and raised people to life. God was telling mankind to take note, to stop and consider the implications.

Christ Jesus, the Lamb of God, took away the sin of the world (John 1:29).

But what does this mean? How can an event that occurred 2000 years ago affect me today? It took some time for me to connect Christ's death to my day-to-day life.

When Chris called the radio broadcast, he was struggling to connect the dots as well. One of the apostle Peter's sermons will help us see the connection.

Past, Present, and Future

Peter delivered this sermon to a group of Gentiles gathered in the home of Cornelius, a Roman centurion. The story is recorded in Acts 10.

As a Jew, Peter wasn't supposed to be in that house. He was breaking Jewish law. But he had received a divine summons, delivered by supernatural means. God was up to something.

Cornelius looked at Peter and said, "Now we are all here in the presence of God to listen to everything the Lord has commanded you to tell us" (verse 33).

Peter got right to the point—the good news of peace through Jesus Christ. He told them of Christ's life, death, and resurrection and added that Jesus was seen by witnesses. He concluded, "All the prophets testify about him that everyone who believes in him receives forgiveness of sins through his name" (verse 43).

The message was simple and powerful. The whole group was saved. They believed on the name of Jesus and were given the gift of God's Spirit. They also received forgiveness of sins at that moment.

Forgiveness is a gift that is offered and received at the moment of salvation.

Have you believed in Jesus Christ? What did you receive at that moment of belief? You received forgiveness of sins.

This forgiveness applies to all of your sins. Paul wrote to the Colossians, "When you were dead in your sins and in the uncircumcision of your flesh, God made you alive with Christ. He forgave us all of our sins" (Colossians 2:13). The word "all" in this verse means all, every one. Every sin you will commit in your lifetime has been forgiven through the shed blood of Jesus Christ.

As a child of God, you have forgiveness for all your sins—past, present, and future. This is a gift of grace.

You may be wondering how this forgiveness can apply to sins you have yet to commit. If so, consider this situation. Let's say tomorrow at ten, you tell a lie. That is a sin, right? One that deserves punishment. Who took the punishment for you? When? Once the lie flows through your lips, you will realize that the sin you just committed was included in that gift of forgiveness you received when you believed in Jesus.

Here is the good news. Jesus shed his blood for every sin you will commit. The Bible is very clear on this. The writer of Hebrews makes the case.

> For Christ did not enter a sanctuary made with human hands that was only a copy of the true one; he entered heaven itself, now to appear for us in God's presence. Nor did he enter heaven to offer himself again and again, the way the high priest enters the Most Holy Place every year with blood that is not his own. Otherwise Christ would have had to suffer many times since the creation of the world. But he has appeared once for all at the culmination of the ages to do away with sin by the sacrifice of himself. Just as people are destined to die once, and after that to face judgment, so Christ was sacrificed once to take away the sins of many; and he will appear a second time, not to bear sin, but to bring salvation to those who are waiting for him (Hebrews 9:24-28).

Jesus Christ entered heaven on your behalf, offering himself once for all. He was sacrificed one time, not again and again. In that one sacrifice, he offered his blood to the Father as payment for your sins. All of them. God the Father accepted Jesus's blood as sufficient to pay your sin debt in full. This is why Jesus cried out in victory, "It is finished." If your future sins weren't included, he would have to die again. That will never happen.

There is nothing left to be done. The gift of forgiveness you received at salvation is complete.

This truth started to erase Chris's fears and doubts and break the grip of sin in his life. We'll talk more about this in chapter 8. For now, let John's words encourage your heart: "I am writing to you, dear children, because your sins have been forgiven on account of his name" (1 John 2:12). They've been forgiven because God is a God who forgives.

7

From Fear to Faith

From the first word out of her mouth I knew the conversation was going to be tense. Barbara was not happy with what she was hearing on the radio broadcast. As a matter of fact, she was downright mad.

The subject for the day was the new covenant, and specifically, the fourth promise of the new covenant: "'Their sins and lawless acts I will remember no more.' And where these have been forgiven, sacrifice for sin is no longer necessary" (Hebrews 10:17-18).

This promise is the explanation of Jesus's victory cry, "It is finished." Jesus's accomplishment, or as one writer put it, his achievement, means your sins are no longer an issue to God. They've been forgiven. Nothing more needs to be done.

From a human perspective, this doesn't sound right. Isn't there something we need to do when we sin? This was Barbara's beef.

"When we sin," she argued, "we are supposed to say we are sorry and ask God to forgive us." This response seems appropriate in our way of thinking. Here is the problem. Grace does not conform to our way of thinking.

Nothing is wrong with telling God you're sorry for your sin. You can ask God to forgive each and every sin as well. However, the sorrow in your heart and the confession on your lips does not bring about God's forgiveness. If they did, forgiveness would cease to be an act of God's grace.

As we learned in chapter 6, forgiveness of sins has already been given to every believer. Paul put it this way: "In him we have redemption through his blood, the forgiveness of sins, in accordance with the riches of God's grace that he lavished on us" (Ephesians 1:7-8). Are you in Christ? If so, what do you presently have? Redemption, the forgiveness of sins. And this is in accordance with God's grace.

Paul opened his letter to the Ephesians giving praise to "the God and Father of our Lord Jesus Christ, who has blessed us in the heavenly realms with every spiritual blessing in Christ" (Ephesians 1:3). Redemption and forgiveness are included in this list.

Jesus already dealt with your sin. He took the punishment and forgave you once and for all.

In Christ, you are a forgiven person.

This should be good news. But for some, it sounds too good to be true. They interpret this as a license to sin. That is how Barbara was hearing it. "You are basically saying you can go out and do anything you want to do."

No, that is not the message of the cross, nor is that grace.

But what about Barbara's concerns? We all still sin. Isn't there something we are supposed to do when sin does occur in our lives? This was the question that troubled my heart for many years. As I said earlier, I received Christ when I was twelve. For the next eight years, my thoughts about God and Christianity and faith in Jesus were all directed toward finding answers to two questions:

> How do I stop sinning?
> What am I supposed to do when I sin?

Since I couldn't stop sinning, I was really more concerned with the second question. Like Barbara, I strongly believed I was supposed to confess, repent, and then ask God to forgive me. And if I really meant it, God would forgive my sin. But I was never sure he had. My formula for forgiveness didn't work. It merely trapped me in a vicious cycle that started shortly after I received Christ at that church camp.

Binaca

Binaca is a breath freshener. Today, it is sold as a spray and as drops. In my seventh-grade year, Binaca was available only as drops. Drugstores and convenience stores displayed it right next to the checkout counter. For a group of boys in a shoplifting gang, stealing Binaca was quite the challenge—one I embraced on numerous occasions.

One Friday, I spent the night with my friend David. Our fun for the evening was stealing Binaca and a lock from the local convenience store. I have no earthly idea why we did this. Maybe it was the challenge—could we get away with it? And we did, or at least I thought we did.

Like a dummy, when I left David's house that Saturday morning, I forgot to take the lock with me. After I left, David's mom went into his room to clean up our mess. She found the lock, and like any mom, she was curious. So she asked David about the lock.

David crumbled. I picture him unraveling like an old sweater. The guilt was too much. He blabbed the truth, "We stole it, Mom.

Bob and I stole it." But it got worse. I was the one who pulled the heist, and that's what David eventually admitted.

You can imagine what happened next. David's mom called my mom. That's what moms do. She told my mom the whole story.

The next Monday, while I was delivering papers on my paper route, Mom drove up beside me. I took one look at her and knew something was terribly wrong. I had skipped band practice that day, and I thought that was why she was mad at me. (I've admitted to being a thief and now a truant. I was a mess!)

Mom looked at me and said, "Get in the car." I didn't want to get in her car at all. I offered up every excuse I could think of. Finally she said, "Binaca," and I was done. David's mom told her not only about the lock but also about all the times we had stolen Binaca. This one word shut me up. I couldn't deny my sin. The black mark was there.

Fear gripped my heart. I knew punishment was close at hand. Seeing the look of disappointment on my mom's and dad's faces seemed more than enough. I certainly didn't want to be punished, but I knew I deserved to be.

Here's what my parents did. They put my punishment in the hands of the store managers. My dad took me to every store that I had stolen something from and made me confess my crime to the store manager. Talk about being scared. In my mind, I was already locked up and doing time in the juvenile detention center with no hope of ever seeing the light of day again. Fortunately, the store managers were lenient. All they required me to do was to pay them for the items I had stolen. But making restitution didn't ease my sense of guilt. There was a bigger question.

What was God going to do to me? That was the scariest thought. In my mind, God had to do something to me because sin can't go unpunished. I started wondering if there was anything I could do to erase that black mark beside my name and get back into God's good graces.

From that point forward, a pattern developed in my life. The pattern always started with a sin. The sin caused guilt and an intense fear of punishment. Out of this fear of punishment, I pleaded with God for forgiveness and promised him I would do better. And then the next sin came. I repeated the same process over and over again, but I never felt forgiven. I had done my part, but I was never sure God had done his. My formula for forgiveness didn't ease the guilt or take away the fear.

Soon I wondered if I was even saved.

So I added to the formula. Confess, repent, ask God for forgiveness...*and ask him to come back into my life*. During my teenage years, I probably asked Christ to come into my life more than 500 times. It was like my heart was a revolving door.

Christianity cannot be reduced to a formula. That's not how faith operates. Every time I sinned, I relied on my faithful execution of the formula to move God to forgive me and assure me that I was saved. I fully believed that if I didn't work myself through this process, my sin would not be forgiven.

This alone shows the importance of forgiveness and how desperately we long to have it. I was trying to earn something that had already been given to me by grace. When I believed on Jesus's name, I received the gift of forgiveness. God placed me in Christ, and in him, redemption, the forgiveness of sins, was mine.

Why was I exhausting myself trying to do anything and everything I could to get God to erase the black mark from beside my name? As I look back on those days, I see two reasons. First, I didn't know the truth. Second, I was afraid. I was afraid of God and afraid that one day he would unleash all his anger on me.

Have you ever thought that? Have you ever looked deep inside and recognized fear as the driving force in your life?

If so, here is something to take note of. Fear turns grace into a reward. This is why I never felt forgiven. I could never do enough in my mind to earn God's forgiveness. This is not the way of grace.

The Fear Factor

Being controlled by fear is devastating. It is the natural consequence of sin. We first see this in the Garden. After Adam and Eve ate the forbidden fruit, they hid from God. When God called out to Adam, Adam responded, "I heard you in the garden, and I was afraid because I was naked; so I hid" (Genesis 3:10). Adam and Eve had never known fear, but when sin entered in, fear suddenly controlled their lives. This fear became a part of our makeup as humans. Sin wrote it into our spiritual DNA. The writers of the New Testament provide keen insight as to why fear is such a big factor in our lives.

I'll let Paul lead on this subject. He analyzes the problem this way: "Once you were alienated from God and were enemies in your minds because of your evil behavior" (Colossians 1:21). This is a vivid description of the lost condition. Evil behavior alienated us from God and caused us to think of him as our enemy. Notice the cause. Evil behavior, what the Bible calls sin, was and is the problem. Remember, Adam and Eve chose to eat from the tree of the knowledge of good and evil. Their choice led to evil behavior. The root of their sin was the choice to believe the serpent's lie. The result was evil behavior. Sin is unbelief. That was the choice Adam and Eve made. Sin originates with unbelief and is defined as evil behavior.

Sin can cause believers to look at God the same way. That's the truth, isn't it? When I first read Colossians 1:21, things started making sense to me. I was letting sin and fear and wrong thinking dictate how I approached God. When you think he is your enemy, you tread lightly.

Here is the good news. God is not now and never was your enemy. If you need to be convinced, take another look at the cross. "In this is love," John wrote, "not that we have loved God but that he loved us and sent his Son to be the propitiation for our sins" (1 John 4:10 ESV). This act reconciled you to God to "present you holy in his sight, without blemish and free from accusation" (Colossians 1:22). God loves you, and the grace he lavished on you to provide redemption, the forgiveness of sins, is the proof.

When I wasn't sure my sins were forgiven, it was hard for me to believe this was true. My relationship with God was built on my fear. With every sin, this fear grew stronger inside me.

I felt that God was going to punish me at any time. I didn't know how—I just knew God's punishment was up ahead. Maybe you've felt the same way. Our minds come up with all kinds of ideas as to what the punishment might be. Loss of job. Financial reversal. Death of a loved one. A devastating illness or injury that happens to us or to someone in our family. The list goes on and on.

This kind of thinking reveals that we don't fully understand the nature of sin and the punishment God requires. "The wages of sin is death" (Romans 6:23). Nothing else will do. That's what we are ultimately afraid of. Jesus died for us to "free those who all their lives were held in slavery by their fear of death" (Hebrews 2:15).

John had us in mind when he wrote, "There is no fear in love. But perfect love drives out fear, because fear has to do with punishment. The one who fears is not made perfect in love" (1 John 4:18). That was me. As I've learned through the years, fear is where many believers live. Evil behavior stirs this up and causes us to wonder, "How could God love me?"

There is only one way out—the finished work of Jesus Christ.

What If?

Barbara insisted that the formula for forgiveness was the only way to go. With each sin, merely confess, repent, and ask God to forgive you, and forgiveness can be yours. But what if you forget to confess a sin? What if you don't feel sorry or don't ask for forgiveness? What then? Does that sin go unforgiven?

How about this possibility—what if you die right in the middle of a sinful act? What happens then?

These "what if" questions punch all kinds of holes through the forgiveness formula. I've actually heard people say this is where grace comes in. To their way of thinking, grace only covers those sins we forget to confess. I like what John Piper says about this. "If our forgiveness depended on the fullness of the knowledge of our sins, we would all perish. No one knows the extent of his sinfulness. It is deeper than anyone can fathom."[1]

Here are better questions to ask. What if you actually believed that God forgave your sins in Christ? What if you took your stand on the new covenant, which includes God's promise that he remembers your sins no more? What if you genuinely trusted in the blood Christ shed for you once and for all?

From Fear to Faith

God did forgive your sins in Christ. Based on Christ's finished work, God chooses to remember your sins no more. The blood of Christ was and is enough. God's grace has been poured out on you in forgiveness. It is yours.

This is the love of God for you. Let it turn your fear into faith.

The day I fully believed that all my sins were forgiven was the day the love of God broke through to my heart. On that day I knew that I knew that I knew God truly and genuinely loved me. His love started driving out the fear in my heart, just as he promised.

I want this for you.

We started this chapter by asking if there is something we need to do when we sin. I have a better question. What does God do when we sin?

Let me offer seven specific actions God takes on your behalf.

- He reminds you of Christ's death on the cross and the forgiveness you have in him. "I am writing to you, dear children, because your sins have been forgiven on account of his name" (1 John 2:12).

- He assures you that you are a child of God. "The Spirit you received does not make you slaves, so that you live in fear again; rather, the Spirit you received brought about your adoption to sonship. And by him we cry, '*Abba*, Father.' The Spirit himself testifies with our spirit that we are God's children" (Romans 8:15-16).

- He shows you the consequences of your sin and then works in you the desire to be reconciled to those you've hurt. "Love does no harm to a neighbor. Therefore love is the fulfillment of the law" (Romans 13:10). "God disciplines us for our good, in order that we may share in his holiness" (Hebrews 12:10).

- He teaches you to say no to sin. "[Grace] teaches us to say 'No' to ungodliness and worldly passions, and to live self-controlled, upright and godly lives in this present age" (Titus 2:11).

- He encourages you to put off the old and put on the new. "You were taught, with regard to your former way of life, to put off your old self, which is being corrupted by its deceitful desires; to be made new in the attitude of your minds; and to put on the new self, created to be like God in true righteousness and holiness" (Ephesians 4:22-24). (See also Colossians 3:5-14.)

- He works all things together for your good. "And we know that in all things God works for the good of those who love him, who have been called according to his purpose" (Romans 8:28).

- He continues to complete the work he began in us. "He who began a good work in you will carry it on to completion until the day of Christ Jesus" (Philippians 1:6).

God always shows us favor, even when we sin. He never withdraws that favor, or grace. His grace produces in us God's desired effect. As Paul wrote, "God's kindness is intended to lead you to repentance" (Romans 2:4).

Our natural response to God's grace is to confess the sin. But what God really desires for us is to trust and rest in the shed blood of Jesus. We experience salvation by grace through faith, and we experience forgiveness by grace through faith as well.

By grace, Jesus took your sins on himself. By grace, he suffered the punishment you justly deserved. By grace, he offered his blood to the Father on your behalf. By grace, he forgave your sins. Now, through faith, thank Jesus for what he has done and rest confidently in the forgiveness that is yours in him.

If you are still wrestling with what to do when you sin, let faith in the finished work of Christ settle the issue. He has taken away your sins once and for all. This is the subject of the next chapter.

8

They're All Gone

Debt is a big problem in America. I know. It has plagued me most of my adult life. To get out of debt takes hard work, discipline, and tough decisions. Many organizations, such as debt relief agencies and financial ministries, offer assistance for this devastating problem.

For many, the struggle gets overwhelming. No matter what they do, the debt never goes away. It hangs on. And every month, the mountain of bills reminds them of the financial mess they are in.

Wouldn't it be nice if the debt could magically disappear? One day you owe $50,000. The next day the debt is paid in full. Could this ever happen? Unless you win the lottery or rich Uncle Fred leaves you a large sum of money, it's unlikely. Slow and steady wins the financial freedom game. But that doesn't keep us from crying out, "Lord, please take this debt away."

When it gets really tough, we even pray to win the lottery. Go ahead and admit it. You've asked the Lord to make your numbers match the winning numbers. I have. I've even promised to give a big portion of the winnings to ministry in hopes this would persuade God to grant my request.

As to financial debt, there is a way out. There is something you can and should do. Cut up your credit cards. Develop a budget. Slash your lifestyle. Use every dime you can squeeze out of your budget to pay off what you owe. Commit to the plan, and in time the debt is gone. Financial freedom is yours. That's what you do with your debt.

Your sin is a totally different story. You can't do anything to get out from under this heavy burden. Hard work, discipline, and tough decisions will not remove this debt. And all the money in the world and all the good deeds mankind has ever done aren't enough to pay it off. Our efforts don't even put a dent in what we owe. The sins and the guilt and the shame keep piling up.

Our only hope of release is the mercy of God. That mercy is delivered to us through forgiveness.

An Interesting Question

We've spent the past two chapters discussing forgiveness, but what does the word really mean? When you say your sins have been forgiven, what does that mean to you?

This could be more difficult to answer than many people think. Our ideas about forgiveness are collected from various sources—psychology, philosophy, religion, literature, and common sense to name a few. Each has a slightly different take on forgiveness. This wide assortment of viewpoints muddies the waters. Where do we turn for help and clarity? Some folks head straight to their good old dictionary.

Here is the definition they find in the Merriam-Webster online dictionary:

forgive *verb* | for·give | \fər-'giv, för-\

: to stop feeling anger toward (someone who has done something wrong) : to stop blaming (someone)

: to stop requiring payment of (money that is owed)

The Merriam-Webster website asks, "What made you want to look up *forgive*?" When I checked, 67 people had posted responses. Here are three comments that caught my attention.

- "'Forgive' is a verb. Verbs require action. So to forgive means that I will actually have to put forth effort. I haven't learned how to forgive yet. But I want to."

- "I read the definition of the word 'forgiveness' first because I am struggling with the idea of forgiveness. The definition is to forgive. So I looked up this definition and I am none the wiser. I cannot fathom how to even begin to forgive. I don't believe in God and have absolutely no interest in religious righteousness so I feel doomed to be destined to a life of being a mean, belligerent a**."

- "I wanted to know if I had forgiven others, if I knew what the meaning was, and it seems like I don't have a forgiving bone in my body. I resent to the core those that have wronged/wounded me."

These comments are revealing. Confusion swirls around the concept of forgiveness. People seem to be unsure as to what it really means, and even more, how to carry it out in life. To find out what forgiveness really means, we need to go to the source, to the only one who has the authority to forgive our sins.

Who Can Forgive?

Mark records a fascinating story in the early chapters of his Gospel account. A group of people were gathered at a house in Capernaum to hear Jesus preach. The house was packed—there wasn't room for another person.

After Jesus started preaching, four men arrived carrying their paralytic friend on a stretcher. They had heard about Jesus and his healing touch. This was their opportunity to help their friend. They were determined to find a way to get their friend into that house. The only option they saw was through the roof. They climbed up, cut an opening, and lowered their friend on his stretcher.

This was faith in action. When Jesus saw it, he looked at the paralytic and said, "Son, your sins are forgiven."

Does Jesus's response seem strange to you? Why did he say such a thing? Jesus's statement confused the crowd as well and raised an eyebrow or two. The teachers of the law were offended.

They were thinking, "Why does this fellow talk like that? He's blaspheming! Who can forgive sins but God alone?" (Mark 2:7). Let's stop right there. These teachers of the law packed deep theological truth in that last seven-word question. They clearly understood that forgiveness originates with God. On this point, their theology was correct. Only God has the power and authority to forgive sins. This is why Jesus's statement to the paralytic was so offensive to them. In their minds, an itinerate rabbi was staking claim to God's authority and power and was stepping in to do what only God can do.

Only God can forgive because he is the offended party—the person we ultimately wrong. Our sins are against him. We are in his debt.

The Jewish teachers also knew that God was willing to forgive. The law, and specifically the sacrificial system, revealed this aspect of God's character to them. "You are a forgiving God, gracious and compassionate, slow to anger and abounding in love" (Nehemiah 9:17). This is what they knew about their God. He has made this even more apparent to us through Jesus. God's forgiving character took action. Through Jesus's shed blood, he freely forgave all our sins. And he did so at his initiative, not ours.

Now back to the story. Jesus was not about to let their thoughts go unchallenged. Before these teachers could say a word, Jesus asked them, "Why are you thinking these things?" (Mark 2:8). I wonder if their palms started to sweat or their stomachs started to knot. I think I would have looked like a deer caught in the headlights. Then Jesus pressed his point. "The Son of Man has authority on earth to forgive sins." Jesus, God in human flesh, exercised his authority and power and forgave the paralytic.

What fascinates me about this story is the paralytic's silence. He didn't say a word. He didn't ask Jesus to heal him. He certainly didn't ask Jesus for forgiveness. He wouldn't even have been there if not for the heroic efforts of his four friends. He was at their mercy and Jesus's. Jesus delivered his mercy with four simple words, "Your sins are forgiven." This is grace.

Here is good news. Jesus says the same four words to you. These aren't just nice words to make you feel better about yourself. Jesus is God. When he says your sins are forgiven, they are forgiven.

But what does this really mean? What actually happens when God forgives? Let's find out. We will start by exploring the biblical concept of forgiveness.

Forgiveness Defined

The Greek word for forgiveness is *aphiemi*. This word appears in various forms 133 times in the New Testament, but it's translated as "forgive," "forgiven," or "forgiveness" on only 36 of those occasions. This fact shocked me. You would think that every time this word showed up in the Greek text, it would be translated as one of those three words. But that's not the case. Seventy-three percent of the time, the word is translated as something else.

For example, in 1 Corinthians 7:10-13, it is translated "divorce." "A husband must not divorce his wife." This caught my interest. In forgiveness, God has actually divorced us from our sins. In Matthew 27:50, it is translated "gave up." "And when Jesus had cried out again in a loud voice, he gave up his spirit." Seeing the different ways the word is used actually gives us a more detailed picture of forgiveness.

According to *The Complete Word Study Dictionary*, the primary meaning of *aphiemi* is "to send forth or away, to let go from oneself."

It also means to dismiss, or put away; to let go from one's power or possession, to let go free, to remove; and to let go from one's further notice, care, attendance, occupancy—that is, to leave or let alone.

You can see how this word can be used in multiple ways. What does this tell us about the true nature of forgiveness?

Based on this definition, let's ask this question. What does God do when he forgives our sins? In other words, what does he do with our sins?

Off They Go!

He Removes Our Sins from Us

He actually took them away from us and placed them on Jesus. In the Old Testament, sins were ceremonially transferred to the animal that was to be sacrificed, such as a bull or goat. This is a beautiful picture of the real transfer of sins from us to Jesus Christ. Paul described it this way in 2 Corinthians 5:21: "God made him who knew no sin to be sin for us, so that in him we might become the righteousness of God."

In this sense, forgiveness is like a divorce. We were connected to our sins—married to them, if you will. That's not a good relationship at all. Sins do not make for good soul mates. They want to control us. Jesus made this point to the Pharisees, but it fell on deaf ears. As we saw in the introduction, he said, "Everyone who sins is a slave to sin" (John 8:34). In forgiveness, God severs the tie and frees us to be joined to him.

He Sends Our Sins Away

God removes our sins from us, and then he sends them away. Where are your sins right now? According to the Word of God, "as far [from you] as the east is from the west." The law provides a beautiful picture of this truth.

On the Jewish calendar, the tenth day of the seventh month was marked as the Day of Atonement. This was the only day of the year the high priest could enter the Most Holy Place to make atonement for himself and for the people of Israel. The process the priest followed was elaborate. Leviticus 16 gives all the details.

Before the priest could give attention to the sins of the people, he first had to atone for his own sins. This required the blood of a bull. Once that sacrifice was made, he could then atone for the sins of the people. To do so, he would take two male goats from the community of Israel and cast lots to determine which goat to sacrifice and which goat to use as the scapegoat.

Once the lots had been cast, he would take the blood of the goat he slaughtered behind the curtain and sprinkle it on the mercy seat. Interestingly, this blood cleansed and consecrated the temple "from the uncleanness of the Israelites" (Leviticus 16:19). Once this was done, he presented the live goat. I'll let Moses describe what the priest was to do next.

He is to lay both hands on the head of the live goat and
confess over it all the wickedness and rebellion of the
Israelites—all their sins—and put them on the goat's
head. He shall send the goat away into the wilderness
in the care of someone appointed for the task. The goat
will carry on itself all their sins to a remote place; and the
man shall release it in the desert (verses 21-22).

The sins of the people were transferred to the goat's head. And
then the goat was sent away into the wilderness. The scapegoat carried away the sins of the people. That's the picture of forgiveness. As
the writer of Hebrews stated, "The law is only a shadow of the good
things that are coming—not the realities themselves" (Hebrews 10:1).
The scapegoat was symbolic of the real forgiveness we receive in Christ.

Through the shed blood of God's own Son, he sent your sins
away forever.

He Remembers Our Sins No More

The Day of Atonement I just described had its limitations. The
blood of bulls and goats lacked the worth and power necessary to
take away sins. This is a key point in the book of Hebrews, specifically chapter 10. Read what the writer says about those old covenant sacrifices.

- They were repeated endlessly, year after year (verse 1).
  This alone proves their inadequacy.

- They left the people conscious of their sins (verse 2).
  Although the people experienced a temporary reprieve,
  deep within they knew their debt of sin still stood as
  a barrier between them and God. Fear of punishment
  consumed their hearts.

- They served as an annual reminder of sins (verse 3).

  Every year, the cold, dark truth about sin and its consequence—death—was kept alive in their thinking.

No, the blood of bulls and goats wasn't enough. These sacrifices merely provided a rough sketch of what was to come.

Jesus died once. His blood cleansed our conscience "from acts that lead to death, so that we may serve the living God" (Hebrews 9:14). His sacrifice did away with sin permanently (Hebrews 9:26). He carried out the will of his Father. He finished his work.

In Jesus's selfless act, God condemned sin. He judged it and pun-ished it by pouring out his wrath on Jesus. The Lamb of God died in my place and in your place.

Two thousand years ago, God remembered your sins. Because of the worth and power of the blood of Jesus, God remembers them no more. Your debt is paid in full.

This is what God has done with your sins. He removed your sins. He sent them away. He is remembering them no more. This is forgiveness.

This is a gift of grace.

Forgiving Others

If God is the only one who has the authority and power to for-give sins, why does the Bible encourage us to forgive others? That is a good question to think through. In forgiving our sins, God did much more than speak forgiveness into our lives. He sent Jesus to die in our place, to shed his blood for our sins. That was a must. For-giveness is always contingent on the shedding of blood. As I pointed out in chapter 6, "without the shedding of blood there is no forgive-ness" (Hebrews 9:22).

In that sacrifice, he removed our sins, placed them on himself, suffered the punishment for them, sent them away, and then chose to remember them no more. How can we do that? Even if we died for someone else, would our blood be sufficient to take that person's sin away? The answer is a resounding no. We can't do for another person what Jesus Christ did for us.

We can, however, extend grace to another person based on the shed blood of Jesus. This is the nature of Paul's encouragement to the believers in Ephesus and Colossae and to us. In his letter to the Ephesians, Paul wrote, "Be kind and compassionate to one another, forgiving each other, just as in Christ God forgave you" (Ephesians 4:32). To the Colossians he wrote, "Bear with each other and forgive one another if any of you has a grievance against someone. Forgive as the Lord forgave you" (Colossians 3:13).

In both of these verses, Paul uses the word *charizomai*. The root word is *charis*, which means "grace." In this context therefore, to forgive is to willingly extend kindness and favor to another person. Normally, we demand that others come back to us on their knees and ask for mercy before we respond in kindness. That's not the way Christ forgave us. He took the initiative. God's provision always precedes our need. His provision effects change in us.

In kindness, we reach out to those who have offended or wronged us, seventy times seven. We do so on the basis of Christ's shed blood. "God was reconciling the world to himself in Christ, not counting people's sins against them" (2 Corinthians 5:19). The Holy Spirit works this measure of grace into our hearts and empowers us to choose not to count people's wrongs against them. Our forgiveness of others reflects the forgiveness we have in Christ.

As you can see, there is more to forgiveness than meets the eye.

God has done a powerful work for you in Christ. In the next chapter, we will see how his powerful work can free you from the prison of your past.

For now, listen again to the words of Jesus to the paralytic. "Your sins are forgiven." This is Jesus's message to you.

9

Let Go

I meet people all the time who say, "I know God has forgiven me, but I'm having a hard time forgiving myself."

Have you heard people say this? Maybe you are saying this right now. If so, you aren't alone. Many people find it difficult to forgive themselves.

I wish I could point you to a verse in the Bible or a specific passage that teaches self-forgiveness. The Bible never addresses the issue. Jesus never told people they needed to forgive themselves.

You can find numerous suggestions about forgiving yourself on the Internet. For example, the Internet site wikiHow offers a nine-step plan for forgiving yourself. Oprah offers help, as do Deepak Chopra and Dr. Phil. Even Stanford University is weighing in on the subject through the Stanford Forgiveness Project. That a major university would undertake the study of forgiveness and its effects on human beings fascinates me. Their research has led them to this conclusion:

> Forgiveness may be viewed as an analogous example of the ability to see one's life through a positive or healing lens. While the research is only suggestive, it may be that all of us could benefit from training in managing life's inevitable hurts and using forgiveness to make peace with the past. In this way, forgiveness may be, as the religious traditions have been claiming all along, a rich path to greater peace and understanding that also has both psychosocial and physiological value.[1]

Interestingly, all these plans frame the process of self-forgiveness in terms of letting go of bitterness, resentment, anger, shame, and guilt. Letting go of all these intense emotions means you've let go of your past and you've forgiven yourself. The path those nine-and ten-step plans suggest is paved with the ideas of self-love, self-acceptance, and self-affirmation and is traveled through meditation, mantras, therapy, reflection, and acts of atonement. It eventually leads, as Stanford researcher Frederic Luskin concluded, to making peace with the past and viewing one's life through a positive or healing lens.

This sounds good and healthy, but it misses the point. Forgiveness means being released from punishment due to sin. It's rooted in God's grace and holiness. It's God's act in Jesus to satisfy his justice. He does not sweep sin under a carpet, nor does he simply choose to ignore it. He judged our sins and condemned them in Jesus Christ "in order that the righteous requirement of the law might be fully met in us" (Romans 8:4). God did not let our sins go unpunished. It is crucial that we know and understand this gospel truth.

Forgiveness is also God's action in Jesus to justify us. He took our sins away from us and placed them on Jesus. Jesus died for us. We died in him. In this death our sins were sent away once and for all. And through Christ's resurrection, God declares us to be righteous, or justified, in his sight. Romans 4:25 puts this together in one clear, powerful statement: "He was delivered over to death for our sins and was raised to life for our justification."

That's forgiveness. You receive this forgiveness in Christ. It became yours the day you confessed with your mouth that Jesus is Lord and believed in your heart that God raised him from the dead.

I hope you can see that forgiveness is not a human concept. It originated with God, and as we learned in chapter 8, he alone has the authority and power to forgive sins. Our sins put us into someone else's debt. We don't like being in that position. All sins are ultimately against God, so we are in his debt. It is his choice to forgive or not to forgive. He chose to forgive. That's grace.

He accomplished this forgiveness through the shedding of blood (Hebrews 9:22). God, in his authority and power, forgave you through the shed blood of Jesus Christ. As C.S. Lewis so eloquently stated, "I think that if God forgives us we must forgive ourselves."

But why do we have such a hard time applying his forgiveness to our lives? Why do we choose to live with guilt and shame? Why does self-condemnation have such a stronghold on us? Why do we continue to allow the sins of our past to tell us who we are today?

The writer of Hebrews offers the answers we need. "See to it that no one falls short of the grace of God and that no bitter root grows up to cause trouble and defile many" (Hebrews 12:15). What is his answer? That we not miss the grace of God. The result of missing God's grace is bitterness, which causes trouble. People who are struggling to forgive themselves are troubled. They are troubled because they carry with them the stains of their past.

There are clear reasons we miss the grace of God. These reasons keep us bound to our past while we stew in bitterness in our present.

I'm Basically Good

If you buy the premise that you are basically good, you will miss the grace of God. If you believe you are fundamentally good, you don't need grace.

Years ago, a renowned radio shock jock made some offensive racial comments on the air. He said them to be funny, but they ended up hurting many people. It took a while for him to recognize how serious his offense was. I think it happened when his company considered firing him.

This provoked a public apology. With cameras rolling, he said; "I have a responsibility to provide a context for who I am and what I do...They need to know that *I am a good person* who said a bad thing, and there is a big difference." To build his case, this radio personality described all the good work he and his wife do for kids with cancer at their ranch in New Mexico. He showed pictures of the children, and then he provided demographic information on the kids he helps. Half are from minority groups.

To drive his point home, he ended his apology with these words, "I don't need a 'come to Jesus' meeting."

This mindset forces you to rationalize your actions, defend yourself, and try to prove to others that indeed you are basically good. Some would call this perfectionism. I believed I was basically good. In those days, I tried to spin my past in a way that would put me in the best light possible. Defending my fragile ego was hard work. It was an endless task. I missed out on truly knowing and experiencing God's forgiveness.

The truth is that we are not basically good. Jesus was very clear on this point: "No one is good—except God alone" (Mark 10:18).

Our hearts were, as Jeremiah wrote, "deceitful above all things and beyond cure" (Jeremiah 17:9). But not beyond the cure of God's grace. He justifies the ungodly (Romans 4:5). This is truth that will set you free.

I've Crossed the Line

Some people think they are beyond the forgiveness of God. A gentleman named John was listening to the *Basic Gospel* radio broadcast one day. Something he heard prompted him to call. The shame and guilt in his voice were palpable. I asked him, "John, do you believe you've crossed a line and that there is no hope for you?"

"Yes, that's exactly how I feel."

What a horrible place to be. If you believe your sins are so big that they have exhausted the supply of God's grace, you are doomed to a life of self-condemnation. John was living his life under a blanket of self-condemnation. He had missed the grace of God for him.

I told John about the apostle Paul. He could have easily lived under a blanket of self-condemnation. He blasphemed God's good name and persecuted Christians. As he said to Timothy, he was the chief of sinners. But God exercised unlimited patience with Paul and poured out his grace on him abundantly. John started getting the picture and seeing there was hope for him.

The gospel tells us that God's grace never runs out. It is a limitless supply, which means there is no line you can cross. There is no place you can be that God cannot reach you. Paul knew this to be true.

> The law was brought in so that the trespass might increase. But where sin increased, grace increased all the more, so that, just as sin reigned in death, so also grace might reign through righteousness to bring eternal life through Jesus Christ our Lord (Romans 5:20-21).

Paul isn't saying we should go out and sin more, as some would think. He is simply saying that God's grace is bigger and more powerful than your sin. Consider this. Jesus Christ died not only for your sins but for the sins of the entire world. That's how big his grace is. Then, to prove Jesus's blood was sufficient, God raised him from the dead. Your sin could not keep him in the grave.

I was so glad John called us that day. He learned his sin could not keep Jesus in the grave. This loosened his grip on his self-condemnation and enabled him to receive God's forgiveness in full.

You see, grace takes you out of your sin and places you in Christ Jesus. This is the place where God no longer remembers your sins (Hebrews 10:17). Since God does not remember your sins, there is no need for you to keep dredging them up. In Christ there is no condemnation (Romans 8:1). If God doesn't condemn you, there is no need to condemn yourself. You can set your heart at rest in his presence (1 John 3:19-20).

I am Unworthy and Unlovable

We've all heard the story of the prodigal son.

He convinced his dad to give him his inheritance so he could go out into the world and make his mark. He set out ready to take on whatever the world threw at him. The world with all of its seductive charms lured him into a life of recklessness and waste. Before long, all his money was gone.

When a famine hit, the only work he could find was feeding pigs. He was at rock bottom. As the story goes, he finally came to his senses and decided to go back home. He worked up a speech for his dad. "Father, I have sinned against heaven and against you. I am no longer worthy to be called your son; make me like one of your hired servants" (Luke 15:18-19).

His wild living made him feel unworthy and unlovable. In his poverty, he felt like a servant and not a son. Many people relate to the prodigal son. Like him, they feel unworthy of God's love.

We get to those feelings of unworthiness in one of two ways. The first follows the path of the prodigal son. Wild, reckless living can create feelings of unworthiness deep within our souls. Unworthiness gives rise to guilt and shame. Shame is that fear of being disgraced if anyone finds out our real story.

My friend Lee was like that. When I first talked with him, he told me, "Bob, I was a very bad guy. I mean a very, very bad guy." He felt unworthy of God's love.

Others feel unworthy because they've been damaged by something that happened to them, or they believe they were the cause of a hurtful situation. They were molested as a child, or abandoned by their parents, or rejected by someone they loved. Or they might believe they were the cause of their parents' divorce or the reason a brother or sister died. These events and beliefs enclose people in a shell of unworthiness. That shell is hard and rigid, it's seemingly impenetrable, and it provides a shield for them to hide behind.

The truth is that none of us are worthy of God's love. He chooses to love us in spite of all that we are. His choice makes us worthy. His choice makes us lovable.

It's scary to let go of the shell, to step out from behind those feelings. God knows your real story. He is not ashamed of you. For proof, look at the cross. His choice to love you was presented in full measure there. It was poured out in grace and mercy. Let go of the shell and let the forgiveness of God cleanse your soul. Faith says it's worth the risk.

Let God throw a party on your behalf.

I'm Not Who You Say I Am

A part of being human is reliving the past. At family gatherings, we tell old stories. They usually start with, "Do you remember when…" When we meet with old friends, we almost immediately jump back into the good old days and talk about life back then. Whenever I meet up with one of my fraternity brothers, my mind gets transported back to those four years between 1976 and 1980 and all the fun and crazy times we enjoyed in college.

One of my favorite memories happened with my friend Brian. One Tuesday evening at nickel beer night, Brian and I engaged in a spiritual conversation. Neither of us had our full wits about us. With slurred words, I was making the most compelling argument I could for Christianity. At the end of the conversation, I looked at him and said, "Brian, I'm going to save you." I think he laughed, which ended our theological discussion. We have laughed about it since.

You've undoubtedly relived some of your wonderful stories from the past. No doubt, it was a source of great pleasure. It is healthy for us to look back and see where we've come from. Writing this book has been a healthy exercise for me both emotionally and spiritually. I've enjoyed looking back at the stories and events God used to shape and mold who I am today.

Most of us wander back to the past only from time to time. Others of us, however, never get out of the past. They are stuck there. Time has marched on, yet in their minds, time stopped for them at a significant event that happened long ago. Have you met people like that? They may have experienced a positive event, or perhaps it was something tragic. Whatever it was, it continues to have such a strong hold on them that they can't move forward or live in the present.

If you pay attention, you'll see this with many former athletes.

They have a hard time moving past their glory years. In their minds, they are still the elite performers who dazzled fans with their skills and talents and seemingly superhuman abilities. Some even think they could still compete at the highest levels. They hang on to the past because they don't know who they are today. The world isn't cheering for them anymore. So they tune their ears to the cheers of yesteryear and cling to their past accomplishments. They proudly boast, "I'm an ex-jock." It's important for them to stay in the past because in their minds, that's all they have.

I lived in Louisville, Kentucky, for several years. I visited a number of veterans at the veterans' hospital there. These were brave, courageous men who had put their lives on the line in service to our country. They came back from war deeply scarred and traumatized emotionally. These guys struggled with readjusting to normal life. That's why they were in the hospital.

Carrying on a conversation with them was difficult for me. They were absorbed in the past. Day after day, they relived the horrors of their war experience. It looped through their minds like a 3-D movie. They hadn't found a way to turn off the projector.

Those who say they can't forgive themselves are somewhat like these ex-jocks and veterans. They have allowed the sins of their past to define who they are today. Rather than seeing themselves through God's act of grace toward them, they see themselves in light of their sins. They may verbalize their identity in Christ, but in their hearts they are holding tightly to their identity as sinners.

They don't go around broadcasting their self-perception. This is their secret. No one knows they are carrying the label of adulterer or thief or addict. They keep it secret because they are scared to death of how people will react if they find out the "truth." They wear masks to keep people away from the truth. They don't give people a chance to love them for who they really are. They don't give God a chance to love them for who they really are.

But you can't hide behind a mask with God. He knows, and your track record doesn't change what he thinks about you and what he has recreated you to be. The gospel changes who you are. Here is the good news. Your identity changed the moment you trusted Jesus Christ. You were born into the family of God and adopted as a son. You are brand-new and bear the name "child of God."

You may not feel or act like a child of God at times, but that does not change the truth. God is so committed to you knowing your new identity, he sent his Spirit to live in you to make it real in your heart (Romans 8:15-16).

You are forever connected to the love of Jesus Christ. Nothing can separate you from his love. You are a forgiven, totally loved child of God.

My friend John Lynch says, "When I wear a mask, the only thing that gets loved is the mask, not the real me." I encourage you to take the mask off. Take the chance of letting others love you for who you really are. There is nothing to fear. You might find that they will love you more than you ever dreamed or imagined.

God is rifling his grace right at you. Don't miss it. Open your heart and let his forgiveness pour in and free you from your past. Let his grace rip away the guilt and shame. Let his love set you on the path of genuinely living out who you are in Jesus Christ.

10

Rest

Joe showed up every Tuesday. The Bible study was important to him. He came because his marriage was on the rocks. He and his wife were struggling and had been for quite some time. As Joe told it, his wife was fed up with the relationship and wanted a divorce. He was holding on as tightly as he could.

As for the cause of the problems, Joe took a page from Adam's book on marriage. When things start to fall apart, blame the wife. "The woman you put here with me..." (Genesis 3:12). Joe pinned all the blame on his wife. According to him, she was the only one at fault. He genuinely believed their marriage would be just fine if his wife changed.

Joe showed up every Tuesday to equip himself to change his wife.

I pointed this out to him on numerous occasions and told him in very clear terms his strategy would not work. The clues were there to help him see this—the most obvious one was the fact that his wife never attended the study with him. But he was oblivious. After every Bible study, he went home excited to share with his wife the latest golden nugget of truth that would help her become the wife he wanted her to be.

Let me take a quick detour here and offer a word of advice to husbands. It's not your job to fix your wife or to change her. Search the Bible. You will not find "Change your wife, thus saith the Lord." Your role is to love her as Christ loves the church. Assuming the role of Mr. Fix-It will push her away. And besides, what makes you think you can change her when you can't even change yourself?

Back to Joe. I tried to shift his thinking. "Joe," I said, "when you come to Bible study, open your heart to the message God has for you, not the message you think he has for your wife." He acknowledged that this made sense, but it took a long time for it to sink in.

Two years passed. Joe was losing hope for his marriage. Everything he tried widened the gap, moving them further and further apart.

One Tuesday night, after the study, Joe grabbed me to talk. He looked different. He asked me, "Have you guys been teaching this stuff all along?"

"What stuff, Joe?"

"Forgiveness—that Christ has totally forgiven all my sins."

I wanted to hit him. I couldn't believe he asked me that question. Had he not heard anything for the past two years?

Christ's finished work on the cross was front and center every single week. And I talked with Joe one-on-one about Jesus's finished work numerous times. The message was being delivered, but he wasn't hearing.

Joe was obsessed with his marriage. He was afraid of losing his wife, but even more, he worried that God would punish him if his marriage failed. That's what was keeping him up at night. Since he believed his wife was the reason the marriage could fail, Joe channeled all of his efforts toward controlling and changing her. He completely missed the message God had for him. The apostle Peter clearly identified Joe's problem.

> If you possess these qualities [faith, goodness, knowledge, self-control, perseverance, godliness, mutual affection, and love] in increasing measure, they will keep you from being ineffective and unproductive in your knowledge of our Lord Jesus Christ. But whoever does not have them is nearsighted and blind, forgetting that they have been cleansed from their past sins (2 Peter 1:8-9).

"Ineffective and unproductive" aptly describes Joe's efforts toward his marriage. The reason is that he forgot, or maybe he never knew, that his sins were forgiven. That led him to wonder, "How can I ever be accepted by a holy God?"

Joe's idea of God was not much different from the pagan views in the Greek and Roman Empires. The gods are angry and need to be appeased. Joe was doing his best but to no avail. His marriage continued to spiral out of control, and Joe believed God's anger toward him was growing by the minute.

In his mind, he was doomed. There was nothing he could do to hold back the flood of God's anger. Punishment was inevitable. That all changed for Joe in a moment during a Tuesday evening Bible study. The truth broke through. Joe's eyes opened, and he saw clearly that Christ's sacrifice had set him apart as "holy in [God's] sight, without blemish and free from accusation" (Colossians 1:22). Christ had already satisfied the Father on his behalf.

Thomas Schreiner, in the book *The Nature of the Atonement: Four Views*, described the results of Christ's death.

The Father, because of his love for human beings, sent his Son (who offered himself willingly and gladly) to satisfy God's justice, so that Christ took the place of sinners. The punishment and penalty we deserved was laid on Jesus Christ instead of us, so that in the cross both God's holiness and love are manifested.[1]

Joe could finally see beyond God's justice into God's heart of love for him. The veil had been lifted, and God's grace was shining through. Understanding the truth that Jesus Christ satisfied God the Father on his behalf was the truth that changed everything for Joe.

Satisfied

I am a child of the '60s and '70s. Rock and roll was my music. I listened to the Beatles, the Who, the Rolling Stones, and many other bands. My buddies and I listened and then spent hours debating the all-important question: What is the greatest rock-and-roll song of all time? (I still maintain it's "Stairway to Heaven" by Led Zeppelin's Jimmy Page and Robert Plant.)

Many of those songs are still front and center on the music scene today. One song that continues to live is the Rolling Stones' "I Can't Get No Satisfaction." The lyrics strike a nerve. For many, the title alone gives voice to their deepest thoughts about God: "No matter what I do, God is never satisfied with me."

The Bible tells a different story. God is satisfied. The reason has to do with the biblical word "propitiation." When was the last time you used *that* in a sentence? It's not a word we hear very often, if at all. But it packs a powerful punch when it comes to our relationship with Jesus Christ.

The first place we see it in the New Testament is in Paul's letter to the Romans. It comes at a high point in Paul's argument for justification by grace through faith. Here is the passage.

> All have sinned and fall short of the glory of God, and are justified by his grace as a gift, through the redemption that is in Christ Jesus, whom God put forward as a propitiation by his blood, to be received by faith. This was to show God's righteousness, because in his divine forbearance he had passed over former sins. It was to show his righteousness at the present time, so that he might be just and the justifier of the one who has faith in Jesus (Romans 3:23-26 ESV).

God put Jesus forward as a propitiation by his blood. What does this mean? Scholars have debated the answer for years and still do. But here is what we need to know. Propitiation is a God thing. It took place between God the Father and Jesus the Son. The writer of Hebrews marks it as a heavenly transaction: "For Christ did not enter a sanctuary made with human hands that was only a copy of the true one; he entered heaven itself, now to appear for us in God's presence" (Hebrews 9:24).

The end result is this—Jesus's shed blood satisfied the demands of God's justice and holiness. Think about that. The wrath of God directed toward you was fully satisfied by the sacrifice of Jesus Christ. God accepted the blood of Jesus as complete and final payment for your sins.

God is satisfied. Jesus's work achieved its purpose. This is grace. Jesus accomplished for you what you could not accomplish yourself. This means there is nothing for you to do except believe. Again we see that we are justified by grace through faith.

The belief part is directly related to your answer to this question: Are you satisfied with the work of Jesus Christ on your behalf?

God is. Why shouldn't you be?

The night Joe truly heard the message, a sense of satisfaction flooded his soul. A release. He started to relax, something he hadn't done in a long time. How could he? Trying to stave off God's punishment is never-ending work. As the saying goes, there is no rest for the weary. No matter what you do, it is never enough. Your work cannot satisfy the demands of God's justice. That work was given to the Lord Jesus Christ. He accomplished the task.

Something else happened. Joe's countenance changed. Those deep lines from spiritual wear and tear started to fade. He looked more at ease with himself and his situation. His spiritual exhaustion began to give way to spiritual rest. It was happening for Joe just as Jesus promised—"Come to me, all you who are weary and burdened, and I will give you rest" (Matthew 11:28).

This rest is God's desire for you as well. Jesus's invitation is to you. The writer of Hebrews worded the invitation this way: "There is a special rest still waiting for the people of God" (Hebrews 4:9 NLT).

Are you satisfied with the work of Christ on your behalf? If so, you've taken the first step to experiencing this rest.

If you are still wrestling with this idea, here is further proof to help you along the way.

He Sat Down

Recently, an interesting video circulated on social media. The producers created a job listing for a director of operations and posted it online. Then they interviewed a number of applicants by video. For the applicants, the job description was beyond belief. First, it required the person to work 24 hours a day, 365 days a year. The person must be mobile and able to stand for long periods of time. No breaks. No vacation or sick leave. One applicant asked if it was legal to demand so much in a job. Another described it as inhumane. Several applicants asked about the pay. The answer came back, "There is no pay."

To this, every single applicant asked, "Who would do such a job?"

The interviewer assured them that literally billions of people currently occupy this position. Then came the punch line. "They're called moms."

The message hit home. These applicants gained an even deeper love and respect for their moms. It's true, you know—a mom's work is never done.

The same was true of the Old Testament priests. Their work was never done. The writer of Hebrews tells us what it was like for the priests. "Day after day every priest stands and performs his religious duties; again and again he offers the same sacrifices, which can never take away sins" (Hebrews 10:11). How would you like to be born into that bloodline? You stand to do a job day after day, again and again, and you never accomplish your purpose. You do that until you turn 50, and then the next generation steps in to carry on the work. Such was the fate of the priests.

But not Jesus. "He is the radiance of the glory of God and the exact imprint of his nature, and he upholds the universe by the word of his power. After making purification for sins, he sat down at the right hand of the Majesty on high" (Hebrews 1:3 ESV). Unlike the priests, Jesus sat down once his work was finished.

The writer of Hebrews didn't want his readers to miss this point. For example, when comparing Jesus to the priests, he explained that Jesus "has no need, like those high priests, to offer sacrifices daily, first for his own sins and then for those of the people, since he did this once for all when he offered up himself" (Hebrews 7:27 ESV). Concerning the sin issue, there is no need for Jesus to get up from his seated position.

Later we read this: "But when Christ had offered for all time a single sacrifice for sins, he sat down at the right hand of God" (Hebrews 10:12 ESV). The message is clear and strong. Jesus sat down because his work was finished. Jesus sat down because his blood satisfied the justice of God. He sat down because propitiation was accomplished. He successfully turned aside the wrath of God.

This means you can rest from all your efforts to appease God and turn away his wrath. "For whoever has entered God's rest has also rested from his works as God did from his" (Hebrews 4:10 ESV).

The Justifier

Through Christ's act of propitiation, God showed us that he is just. He dealt with our sin. He didn't ignore it or sweep it under a heavenly carpet. He judged it, he condemned it, and he punished it. All obligations were fully satisfied. But that was not the end goal.

God is both just and the justifier. He freely justifies "those who have faith in Jesus" (Romans 3:26). That includes you.

God didn't just take away your sins—he also declared you to be righteous. This is the proof that your sins have been forgiven and that God is fully satisfied with you. This means you are in right standing with God. You didn't work your way to that status. God justified you freely by his grace.

Let's think about how this truth plays out in daily living. We still sin, don't we? And each sin we commit, no matter how big or small, deserves punishment. That punishment is death.

Now, our legal system presumes the innocence of every person accused of wrongdoing. The prosecution bears the responsibility of proving beyond a reasonable doubt that the accused person is guilty.

In God's court, the prosecution presented ample evidence, and all were found guilty. The presumption of innocence does not apply. All are subject to punishment. We know this intuitively. As Paul argued in Romans, the requirements of the law are written on our hearts. Our consciences bear witness to this fact and our thoughts accuse us (Romans 2:15).

As we have seen, "the wages of sin is death" (Romans 6:23). This is the punishment we deserve. Yet God says to those who are in Christ, "Your sins have been forgiven." How do we know punishment is not waiting for us sometime in the future?

Justification is God's answer.

God justifies sinners and declares them right in his sight on the basis of Christ's finished work on the cross. This is the point Paul made in Romans 3, which we looked at earlier, and it's the point he amplifies in Romans 4.

> What does the Scripture say? "Abraham believed God, and it was credited to him as righteousness."
>
> Now to the one who works, wages are not credited as a gift but as an obligation. However, to the one who does not work but trusts God who justifies the ungodly, their faith is credited as righteousness (Romans 4:3-5).

When Joe trusted Jesus Christ, God's righteousness was credited to his account. Believing and resting in this truth freed Joe to trust Jesus to work in his marriage situation. That was a 180-degree turn in his relationship with Christ.

Before, he was doing everything he could to keep God from being mad at him. He was basically working on his own, as if he were outside of God's presence. Now he was going boldly into the throne of grace to receive mercy and find grace to help him in his time of need (Hebrews 4:16).

Jesus doesn't want us to be afraid of him when problems arise. He wants us to trust in him and depend on him. When we do, we can watch him work all things together for our good. We can trust him because he satisfied the law on our behalf. His punishment was our punishment. In exchange, his righteousness became our righteousness. So as we've seen, God is both just and the one who justifies those who have faith in Jesus Christ.

The fact that God has declared us righteous in his sight is proof that all our sins have been forgiven. When I say all, I mean sins of the past, present, and future. They have been sent away from us as far as the east is from the west, and righteousness has been credited to our account. On the basis of Jesus's shed blood, God treats us as if we had never sinned.

Consider this question. What would happen to the righteousness that was credited to your account if one sin had been left unpunished? God in his justice would have to withdraw his righteousness and treat you as a guilty sinner, which means he would punish you for that one sin.

Aren't you glad Jesus died for all your sins? His blood satisfied the law for every sin you have committed or will commit. Jesus took them all.

As a result, God says to you, "There is therefore now no condemnation for those who are in Christ Jesus. For the law of the Spirit of life has set you free in Christ Jesus from the law of sin and death" (Romans 8:1-2 esv).

In part three, we will see what it means to be free in Christ. Spoiler alert. The good news keeps getting better.

Part 3

Freedom

If you believe on the Lord Jesus Christ you are free.

D.L. MOODY

You Are Free

Forgiveness plus life equals freedom. Real freedom.

This is where the gospel takes us. Paul put it this way: "It is for freedom that Christ has set us free" (Galatians 5:1). To the question, "What is God's will for my life?" freedom is God's answer.

It's what you have longed for all your life. Now it's yours.

But here is the reality. Freedom can be scary. When asked about the idea, Robert Capon, an Episcopal priest and author, made this point: "One of the problems with any authentic pronouncement of the gospel is that it introduces us to freedom."[1]

What will you do with your newfound freedom? How will you respond?

Legalism doesn't think you will handle it very well at all. It fears you will go wild without its control in your life. Subtly and not so subtly, legalism delivers the message, "You can't handle freedom."

What I mean by legalism is this: anything man does through human effort to earn God's love and acceptance. Legalism is a works-based approach to God. Works, not grace through faith, mark the path to righteousness. Paul described this system concisely in his letter to the Romans, as we saw in chapter 10: "Now to the one who works, wages are not credited as a gift but as an obligation" (Romans 4:4).

But there is no way for us to earn righteousness. This is impossible. The only things we earn through this works-based system are condemnation and death.

Through faith in Jesus we've escaped that system. We are not under law. We are under grace. We've been set free.

Even so, the imprint of legalism still remains. When circumstances get tough, or when the temptations of the world and the desires of the flesh get strong, legalism tries to take control. The world is filled with evidence that suggests we listen to the voice of legalism and let it have a say in how we live our lives.

The prime example is recidivism rates for US prisoners. What happens once prisoners are released from prison? How do they handle their newfound freedom? In 2005, the Bureau of Justice launched a five-year study to find the answers. They followed 405,000 prisoners who were released in 30 states. Here are the findings.

> An estimated two-thirds (68 percent)…were arrested for a new crime within three years of release from prison, and three-quarters (77 percent) were arrested within five years, the Bureau of Justice Statistics (BJS) announced today.

> More than a third (37 percent) of prisoners who were arrested within five years of release were arrested within the first six months after release, with more than half (57 percent) arrested by the end of the first year.[2]

These statistics are alarming. They give credence to the idea that we can't handle freedom. As a parent of three kids, I understand.

Jeanna and I are in the letting-go stage of parenting. Our oldest, Caitlin, has already left the nest. Our son, Coleman, will soon leave us with another empty room in the house as he goes out to find his way in the world. McKenzie, our youngest, is not far behind. For Jeanna and me, this is a struggle. We do not want to let them go.

What if they make mistakes? What if they don't make the choices we want them to make? Just asking these questions surfaces all of our parental control tendencies. But we can't act on these impulses. If we do, we will keep our kids as children, rather than releasing them into adulthood. That would be downright cruel.

Legalism is a cruel parent. It doesn't want to release us into adulthood. It would lose control if it did. No, legalism wants to keep us behind bars. It assumes that its protective custody is the only safe place for us to be.

But God thinks differently. Freedom is his goal for us, and he has equipped us to handle it. This was foreshadowed in one of the most familiar stories in the Old Testament.

A Plot Gone Bad

Israel was a slave nation for four hundred years, from around 1900 to 1500 BC. You are probably familiar with the story.

Jacob, the grandson of Abraham, fathered twelve sons. Joseph, the eleventh of the bunch, was his favorite. This irked his ten older brothers. Joseph's dreams didn't help his situation with his brothers either. If you put yourself in their shoes, you can see why. Joseph had two vivid dreams that he shared with his brothers. In each, Joseph was in the middle with everything else in the dream bowing down to worship him. Now, to his brothers, he was simply rubbing their noses in his status as the favorite son. They didn't like it at all. They were already jealous of Joseph. This ratcheted that up to hatred.

Hatred and jealousy are powerful forces. They can make a person do unthinkable acts. For Joseph's brothers, their hatred and jealousy led them to hatch a plot for his murder. Only one of the brothers recoiled at this. Reuben, the oldest, took a stand. He wanted to rescue Joseph and deliver him back to Jacob.

Judah had another idea. "Let's sell him." The patriarch sells his own brother into slavery. (Interestingly, Jesus is from Judah's line. The patriarch's seed rescues us from slavery and sets us free.)

Judah's brothers agreed to his plan. When a caravan of Ishmaelites approached the fields where they were tending their flocks, the brothers took action. "So when the Midianite merchants came by, his brothers pulled Joseph up out of the cistern and sold him for twenty shekels of silver to the Ishmaelites, who took him to Egypt" (Genesis 37:28).

The favorite son was now a slave living in a foreign land. Matters got worse for Joseph. A scandalous incident contrived by Potiphar's wife landed him in prison. The stage was being set for the fulfillment of God's words to Abraham: "Then the LORD said to him, 'Know for certain that for four hundred years your descendants will be strangers in a country not their own and that they will be enslaved and mistreated there'" (Genesis 15:13). A sibling rivalry started the ball rolling. Climate change, in the form of a drought and famine, wrote the next act.

Joseph's situation changed dramatically. His meteoric rise from slave to ruler was miraculous. Pharaoh was troubled by a dream, but none of his magicians or wise men could interpret it for him. Pharaoh's cupbearer told him about a young Hebrew prisoner who had accurately interpreted one of his own dreams. Pharaoh immediately sent for Joseph.

God gave Joseph the meaning. Seven years of prosperity would be followed by seven years of drought. After giving the interpretation, Joseph sketched out a plan to prepare for the coming famine. Pharaoh, impressed by Joseph's wisdom, said, "I hereby put you in charge of the whole land of Egypt" (Genesis 41:41).

The famine devastated not only Egypt but Canaan as well. So Jacob sent his sons to Egypt to buy food. Unbeknownst to them, the Egyptian-looking official they met with was Joseph himself. He persuaded his brothers to bring Jacob and all of their families to Egypt to live. Sixty-six people in all moved from Canaan. Joseph arranged for them to settle in Goshen.

There, these 66 people mushroomed into a small nation. They "became so numerous that the land was filled with them" (Exodus 1:7). The great number of Israelites alarmed the new king of Egypt. To control them, he put slave masters over them. Once favored because of Joseph, the Israelites were now slaves in a foreign land and subjected to forced labor and ruthless treatment.

For four hundred years, the Israelites suffered at the hands of the Egyptians. They were living in the wrong place, under the control of the wrong person, carrying out the wrong purpose. But God did not leave them there. He heard their cries. He elevated one from within their ranks to lead them to freedom.

A Powerful Promise

Moses was that man. He was a Levite but was raised as an Egyptian under the care of Pharaoh's daughter. At the age of 40, he witnessed a fight between an Egyptian and a Hebrew. Moses killed the Egyptian. When word of this reached Pharaoh, he tried to kill Moses, but Moses escaped and fled to Midian. That's where God appeared to him in a burning bush.

God revealed his plan to rescue his people. Moses was his man to orchestrate the escape. Moses wasn't so sure he was the right choice. "'Who am I that I should go to Pharaoh and bring the Israelites out of Egypt?' And God said, 'I will be with you'" (Exodus 3:11-12).

Let's stop right here for just a moment. The Israelites' world was about to be rocked. God's power and presence were about to sever them from the only life they had ever known. Every step they would soon take would be a step into the unknown. Granted, they were sick and tired of Egyptian oppression. They wanted to be free. But to experience freedom, everything had to change.

In a five-word promise, God injects the most powerful motivator of all—hope. God's power and presence would shape their new world. They would not be alone to fend for themselves. I AM WHO I AM would lead the charge out of slavery and into the Promised Land. He was their hope.

The same is true of you. Paul put it this way: "To them God has chosen to make known among the Gentiles the glorious riches of this mystery, which is Christ in you, the hope of glory" (Colossians 1:27). Jesus Christ delivered you out of darkness. He set you free by unlocking the chains of sin and death that held you captive. He didn't leave you to figure out this newfound freedom on your own. He came to live inside you. Your hope of living life to the full is anchored to his power and presence in you.

This hope trumps fear. And it silences all those legalistic voices, both the internal and external ones, that say you can't handle freedom. Christ in you says you can!

The Exodus

Pharaoh was stubborn. He was not going to let the Israelites go. They were far too valuable to him and the Egyptian economy. Through a series of plagues, God displayed his awesome power.

With each one, Pharaoh's heart hardened even more. Even after God darkened the sky for three days, Pharaoh still refused to let the Israelites go.

God warned Pharaoh of what was next—the death of every firstborn in Egypt. God's judgment on Egypt and its gods was soon to be complete. The angel of death was to go through the land and kill every firstborn male, both human and animal. To spare the firstborn sons of the Israelites, God instructed them to sacrifice an unblemished lamb and spread the blood on the sides and tops of the doorframes. When the angel saw the blood, he would pass over that house, sparing those inside.

The blood of the lamb. As we learned earlier, Jesus's blood turned God's wrath from us. The Passover foreshadowed Christ's work on our behalf.

At midnight, God swept through Egypt, striking down all the firstborn. The land was filled with wailing. Pharaoh finally had enough. He called for Moses and Aaron in the middle of the night and said to them, "Up! Leave my people, you and the Israelites! Go, worship the LORD as you have requested" (Exodus 12:31).

Six hundred thousand men, along with women and children, gathered their belongings and all they had plundered from the Egyptians, and they left. It was 430 years to the day from when they first arrived in Egypt. Remember this number. We will look at its significance in chapter 13.

God led the people south toward the Red Sea. Just as he promised Moses, he was with them.

> By day the LORD went ahead of them in a pillar of cloud
> to guide them on their way and by night in a pillar of
> fire to give them light, so that they could travel by day
> or night. Neither the pillar of cloud by day nor the pillar

of fire by night left its place in front of the people (Exodus 13:21-22).

After the Israelites fled, Pharaoh reconsidered what he had done. He gathered his armies and chariots, pursued the people of God, and overtook them at their camp near the Red Sea.

The Israelites were terrified. When fear hits, we lose perspective on all that God has for us both now and in the future. We want to go back to what was comfortable, even if it was slavery. The Israelites were no different. They let Moses have it.

> Was it because there were no graves in Egypt that you brought us to the desert to die? What have you done to us by bringing us out of Egypt? Didn't we say to you in Egypt, "Leave us alone; let us serve the Egyptians"? It would have been better for us to serve the Egyptians than to die in the desert! (Exodus 14:11-12).

Every time I read their complaint, I get critical. Doesn't it raise questions in your mind? God was clearly with them, right? Why were they blind to this reality? And didn't they remember all God had done for them to this point? They left Egypt as wealthy people. They were promised a new land and a new way of life. God was guiding every step of their way. He had taken care of their every need and had shown his immense power. What were they missing?

Moses calmed the people. The Lord was about to act again on their behalf and deliver them to safety.

Moses stood at the banks of the Red Sea and raised his staff into the air. The Lord parted the sea. The Israelites "went through the sea on dry ground, with a wall of water on their right and on their left" (verse 22).

When the Egyptians pursued, Moses raised his staff again, and the walls of water covered the dry land. Not one member of the Egyptian army survived. "That day the LORD saved Israel from the hands of the Egyptians" (verse 30). Salvation was theirs.

Three Lessons for Us

What does this story tell us today?

First, it reminds us that salvation is God's work from start to finish. Every aspect of Israel's rescue was carried out by God alone. His power and presence delivered them to safety and freedom. His power and presence in the person of Jesus Christ delivered you to safety and freedom as well. This is grace.

Next, Israel's old way of life came to an end. They were no longer slaves. The Egyptian reign had been buried in a watery grave. I think Paul had this story in mind when he penned these words to the Romans:

> If we have been united with him in a death like his, we will certainly also be united with him in a resurrection like his. For we know that our old self was crucified with him so that the body ruled by sin might be done away with, that we should no longer be slaves to sin—because anyone who has died has been set free from sin (Romans 6:5-7).

Your old way of life has come to an end. You are no longer a slave to sin. You are a child of the living God. But not just a child. God declared you to be a son.

> Because you are his sons, God sent the Spirit of his Son into our hearts, the Spirit who calls out, "*Abba*, Father." So you are no longer a slave, but God's child; and since you are his child, God has made you also an heir (Galatians 4:6-7).

He sees you as an adult, no longer in need of a tutor. He is there with you, working inside you. This equips you to live in freedom.

Finally, in God's presence there is nothing to fear. Yes, freedom can be scary. Everything in the world tries to keep you from it. Even your old legalistic thoughts discourage you from walking that path. Be brave and courageous. Freedom is what you've longed for. It's yours. Every step you take as a child of God, he is there with you.

12

Don't Look Back

I like the word "new." I bet you do too.

It's an exciting word, especially when it's attached to things like cars, clothes, a house, or gadgets. We all like new things and want new things. As a society, we crave the latest and greatest of everything. This desire for "new" has reached a fevered pitch.

Seth Godin, a marketer, author, and blogger, described the craze for new. "There's an increasing desire, almost a panic, for something new. Yesterday was a million years ago, and tomorrow is already here. The rush for new continues to increase, and it is now surpassing our ability to satisfy it."[1]

We like "new" when it comes to our possessions. But that's not the case when it comes to the weightier matters of life. With these, "new" is a scary word. Embracing something new on this front means change. It's a break from the comfort of the status quo, or the way we've always done things. "New" ushers us into the unknown and unfamiliar, and we're not sure what to expect.

It's hard for us to change, to let go of all that is familiar and comfortable. We resist with all our strength and might. This is just part of our human nature.

One Christmas, I asked Mom and Dad for a set of golf clubs. When Christmas day arrived, I woke up early and sneaked downstairs to the living room. There they were, leaning against the wall next to the Christmas tree. I couldn't believe my eyes. I was going to be a golfer.

I didn't know anything about golf other than it looked like fun. I was anxious to try it out. My dad took me to a local course. That first time was so frustrating. The golf ball flew every direction but straight. But I was determined to get good at the game. I didn't take any lessons—I tried to figure it out on my own. Yes, that was a big mistake. There aren't too many self-taught golfers who are very good. I was no exception. For the next 12 years or so, I grooved a very bad golf swing.

After I married Jeanna, she did something very nice for me. She arranged for me to take golf lessons with one of the top ten golf teachers in the world. He videotaped my swing. I don't think I've ever seen anything so awkward in my life. He looked at me and said, "I can help you, but you will need to let go of that old swing." I was fine with that until he started teaching me a new swing. It felt uncomfortable and unnatural. My body fought the changes.

When I went to the course to test out the new swing for the first time, it felt weird. My tendency that round was to go back to my old swing, the one I was used to. And at the end of the round, my score didn't improve. I wanted to give up on the lessons and go back to the golf I knew.

As we saw in the last chapter, that was the Israelites' attitude after they gained their freedom. They wanted to go back to what was familiar. But they couldn't. Their only option was to move forward to the land God had promised them, but their fear of the unknown turned their eyes back to Egypt, back to slavery.

This is why the gospel can be a frightening proposition. Spiritual birth ushers us into the new. Paul made this point clearly: "If anyone is in Christ, the new creation has come: The old has gone, the new is here!" (2 Corinthians 5:17). Ready or not, here it is.

- a new life (Romans 6:4)
- a new identity (John 1:12)
- a new self (Ephesians 4:24)
- a new heart (Ezekiel 36:26)
- a new covenant (Hebrews 9:15)
- a new command (John 13:34)
- a new way (Romans 7:6)

You might not know what this new life in Christ will look or feel like. And at first, it may feel a little awkward or strange. Like the Israelites, you may look back to your old life, especially when you feel down or blue or when you are going through a tough circumstance. At those times, Satan will do his best to make you think your old life was pretty good. "Remember all the fun you had when you...?"

But as Peter wrote, "You have spent enough time in the past doing what pagans choose to do—living in debauchery, lust, drunkenness, orgies, carousing and detestable idolatry" (1 Peter 4:3). It is time to let go of the old, to stop looking back, and to embrace the new.

There is nothing to fear. Jesus Christ is with you. He will never leave you. This means freedom for you, for "where the Spirit of the Lord is, there is freedom" (2 Corinthians 3:17). The "new" that Christ has for you is better than anything you could ever dream or imagine. And besides, you can't go back. Once you are in the light, you can't go back to darkness. Once you have been set free, you will never be a slave to sin and death again. Once you cross over from death to life, the only way is forward in the newness of life.

A Tale of Two Kingdoms

Standing proud in the middle of New York Harbor on Liberty Island is the Statue of Liberty. The statue was a gift of friendship given to the United States by the people of France. This icon of freedom was designed by Frederic Auguste Bartholdi and was dedicated on October 28, 1886.

The statue is a female figure that represents Libertas, the Roman goddess of freedom. She holds a torch in one hand and a tablet in the other. Inscribed on the tablet is July 4, 1776, the date of the Declaration of Independence. At her feet lies a broken chain. On the base is the famous poem "The New Colossus" by Emma Lazarus: "Give me your tired, your poor, your huddled masses yearning to breathe free..."

Lady Liberty welcomes immigrants to the United States. To these immigrants, it represents a better way of life and the promise of freedom. For most of us born in the United States, freedom is all we have ever known. But for many of those who land on our shores, it's a different story altogether. Theirs is a tale of two very different countries.

And so it is for every Christian. Our story is a tale of two kingdoms. It involves a daring rescue mission that snatches us away from one kingdom and places us fully and forever into a new kingdom.

Here is the story as Paul lays it out. "He has rescued us from the dominion of darkness and brought us into the kingdom of the Son he loves, in whom we have redemption, the forgiveness of sins" (Colossians 1:13-14). God rescued you from the dominion of darkness. That's where you once lived. But not anymore—you are now in the kingdom of the Son, a place of love, redemption, and forgiveness.

There is no going back. If you compare the two, you will never want to go back.

The dominion of darkness (that sounds so ominous!) is disguised in glamour and glitz. On the surface everything shines, but that belies all that's underneath. The ruler of the air, Satan himself, oversees all the activities. He operates this kingdom on the principle of deception.

When we lived there, we readily followed his ways and the ways of the world, and we lived to carry out the desires of the flesh. We did so because we were spiritually dead, sinners by name. We lived as condemned people under the control of sin, and eternal death was our destiny. That's the kingdom of darkness.

Jesus entered into that kingdom of darkness to rescue us and fit us to live in his kingdom. As John wrote, "In him was life, and that life was the light of all mankind. The light shines in the darkness, and the darkness has not understood it" (John 1:4-5). His plan was drawn up by love and grace and was carried out through death, burial, and resurrection. Paul explained the intricacies.

> Or don't you know that all of us who were baptized into Christ Jesus were baptized into his death? We were therefore buried with him through baptism into death in order that, just as Christ was raised from the dead through the glory of the Father, we too may live a new life (Romans 6:3-4).

You died in Christ. Everything that was true of you in the

dominion of darkness came to an end. It was buried once and for all. Then you were raised as a new creation in Christ. Now your life is in him. That kingdom of darkness has no hold over you anymore. The power of sin and death has been broken. You are free.

You now belong to Christ. You have a new identity as a child of God. You are under grace and led by the Holy Spirit. Your destiny is with God forever as a citizen of the new heaven and the new earth (Revelation 21:1-4).

Through faith in Jesus Christ, you have gone from darkness to light and from the power of Satan to God. You are in the kingdom of the Son.

The Way of the Kingdom

Okay, so you've been raised to walk in the newness of life. How does that happen? Walking in the newness of life happens through faith, hope, and love. These are the traits that mark every believer. These are the "laws" of the kingdom of God placed in our minds and wrote on our hearts (Hebrews 8:10).

Paul uniquely ties these characteristics together in his letter to the Colossians. The interplay between the three is truly fascinating.

> We always thank God, the Father of our Lord Jesus Christ, when we pray for you, because we have heard of your *faith* in Christ Jesus and of the *love* you have for all God's people—the *faith* and *love* that spring from the *hope* stored up for you in heaven and about which you have already heard in the true message of the gospel that has come to you. In the same way, the gospel is bearing fruit and growing throughout the whole world—just as it has been doing among you since the day you heard it and truly understood God's grace (Colossians 1:3-6).

Hope is the guarantee of what is to come. This hope is tied to the promised Holy Spirit. He is the seal that guarantees our inheritance (Ephesians 1:13-14). He is the one who keeps our eyes squarely on Jesus. He anchors us to all that we are and all that we have in him. We don't fully see these realities, but hope says...

> We are children of God, and what we will be has not yet been made known. But we know that when Christ appears, we shall be like him, for we shall see him as he is. All who have this hope in him purify themselves, just as he is pure (1 John 3:2-3).

From this hope spring forth faith and love. Notice in Colossians that Paul centers Jesus Christ as the object of our faith. "Faith" is not a stand-alone word. It is meaningless apart from Jesus. As Paul wrote, "Faith comes from hearing the message, and the message is heard through the word about Christ" (Romans 10:17).

Let's spend a few minutes dissecting this verse. Before faith came, you lived in the kingdom of darkness as an unbeliever. You lived in unbelief. That was your sin. That was Adam's sin. When tempted, he chose to believe the lie of the serpent. When he did, unbelief became the dominant principle for human existence. Jesus identified this as the sin of the world. Concerning the work of the Holy Spirit, Jesus said, "When he [the Holy Spirit] comes, he will prove the world to be wrong about sin and righteousness and judgment: about sin because people do not believe in me..." (John 16:8-9).

This sin of unbelief attached you to the tree of the knowledge of good and evil. You were left to figure out life through your own understanding and then to carry out the plan through human effort. Basically, your unbelief relegated you to a life of dos and don'ts. The Bible calls that spiritual death.

With that unbelieving heart, you weren't fit for the new life in the kingdom. But things changed when Jesus rescued you.

The message concerning Christ turned your heart from unbelief to belief. The grace of God engendered your response of faith. Again the theme, by grace through faith. This radical change equipped you for life in the kingdom. As Paul wrote to the Galatians, "I have been crucified with Christ and I no longer live, but Christ lives in me. The life I live in the body, I live by faith in the Son of God, who loved me and gave himself for me" (Galatians 2:20). The way of the kingdom is faith.

At first, faith feels strange to us. For so long, all we knew was unbelief. It was ingrained into our minds. Those trails of unbelief we once walked are well worn and familiar. When circumstances get tough, those old paths call to us saying, "This is the way to happiness." Sometimes we listen and move down those paths of darkness. But as soon as we do, we are keenly aware we don't belong there anymore.

Getting drunk with my buddies was a way to happiness for me in college. After my life changed, I traveled down that path a time or two. When I did, I felt out of place. This jarred my memory. Getting drunk never made me happy. It left me feeling guilty and empty on the inside. God rescued me from all that and equipped me to live in the newness of life.

Here is the wonderful news. Faith in Jesus expresses itself in love toward others. He is love. He has come to live inside you. When you abide in him, love is the fruit. Remember, you've been "brought into the kingdom of the Son he loves."

Faith, hope, and love are the way of the kingdom.

Press On

Before I married Jeanna, whenever I felt alone, I started to think about all my old girlfriends. I dated a nurse when I worked at Piedmont Hospital right after I graduated from college. She really liked me. We dated for several months and then stopped. There wasn't a spark. The whole dating thing with her felt awkward and strange. It didn't work out at all, so we quit seeing each other.

Then I moved to Dallas. When I first arrived, I didn't know anyone. For the first three months, loneliness was my constant companion. I remember looking around my apartment one night and thinking, "I could die and no one would know." In those lonely moments, guess who I started thinking about—the nurse. "I wonder what she is doing now. Would she go out with me? We did have some fun." In my loneliness, I tried to track her down. The relationship didn't work the first time. I don't know why I thought it would work the second time. That was crazy thinking.

But we all do it. You've done something like that, right? One of the lessons in life is that we can't go back. The only option is to move forward. I'm glad I did, because I met Jeanna. As we became friends, I realized she was the one for me.

The same is true for the Christian life. Once we are saved, we can't go back. We can't reverse all that Christ accomplished. We can't go from life back to death. We can't go from light back to darkness. And we can't go from belief back to unbelief. Why would we want to?

Paul asked this question: "We are those who have died to sin; how can we live in it any longer?" (Romans 6:2). You died to sin, to unbelief. The old you is gone. You are new in Jesus, equipped to live a life of faith, hope, and love. What does the Scripture say to you? Press on!

The Bible encourages you to take hold of the eternal life to which you were called (1 Timothy 6:12). The Bob Christopher paraphrase reads, "Grab it and live it."

I'm confident Paul had this in mind when he wrote these words:

> Brothers and sisters, I do not consider myself yet to have taken hold of it. But one thing I do: Forgetting what is behind and straining toward what is ahead, I press on toward the goal to win the prize for which God has called me heavenward in Christ Jesus (Philippians 3:13-14).

It sounds so good and so simple. It's what you want. But let me ask, is anything holding you back?

- *Are you fearful of the unknown?* New life is just that— new. That means it's different, unfamiliar. It requires change. Change is not something we take to readily because we are not sure of the benefits. Turn that fear into faith. Trust the One who loves you and gave his life for you. His life is the best—nothing can compare.

- *Are you concerned about what other people will think of you?* Other people's opinions are very important to us. What they think matters. I certainly don't want people to think I'm a religious fanatic. Eric Hoffer wrote, "It's been said that when people are free to do as they please, they usually imitate one another." What really matters is what God thinks. His opinion is better than anyone else's. Trust what he has to say.

- *Do you think the world has something better to offer?* Admittedly, the world is an attractive place on the surface. It markets itself very well. For the longest time I was Mr. Noncommittal. I was always waiting for something better to come along. The world doesn't offer anything that can compare to Christ. The only way to find out is to take hold, jump in, and live.

It takes courage, but experiencing the life of Jesus is worth everything. This is what he saved you for.

13

Living a Sunday Life
in a Friday World

Have you ever heard the sermon "It's Friday, but Sunday's Coming"? I was introduced to this masterpiece in high school. A pastor friend borrowed it for one of his messages. That was almost 40 years ago, and I've never forgotten the message. I found a recording of this sermon on YouTube delivered by the great S.M. Lockridge. I've listened to it literally hundreds of times. I still get goose bumps every time I listen.

The preacher starts softly, "It's Friday...Jesus is praying...Peter is sleeping...Judas is betraying...but Sunday's coming.

"It's Friday," he says again, this time a little louder. "The disciples are running like sheep without a shepherd...Mary is crying...Peter is denying...but they don't know that Sunday's coming."

He keeps repeating the phrase. With every turn, that horrible Friday grows darker and more hopeless.

"It's Friday. See Jesus walking to Calvary...His blood dripping ...His body stumbling...and his spirit is burdened...But, you see, it's only Friday—Sunday's coming.

"It's Friday...The world is winning...People are sinning...And evil is grinning.

"It's Friday...The soldiers nail my Savior's hands to the cross...They nail my Savior's feet to the cross...And then they raise him up next to criminals.

"It's Friday...But let me tell you something...Sunday's coming."

The cadence quickens.

"It's Friday...He's hanging on the cross...Feeling forsaken by his Father...Left alone and dying. Can nobody save him?

"Oh, it's Friday...But Sunday's coming.

"It's Friday...The earth trembles...The sky grows dark...My King yields his spirit.

"It's Friday...Hope is lost...Death has won...Sin has conquered ...And Satan's just a-laughing."

The pastor pauses briefly. His next words are stark, emptied of all emotion.

"It's Friday...Jesus is buried...A soldier stands guard...And a rock is rolled into place."

Friday ends in the worst possible way, but...

"It's Friday. It is only Friday.

"Sunday is coming!"[1]

With those last three words, the pastor fills that darkest day with light and hope.

If you ever hear this sermon, you'll never forget it. To me, it is one of the most powerful evangelistic sermons ever delivered.

Last Easter, I shared it with our fellowship group in Carrollton, Texas. I did so to make this point—Sunday is here.

On that third day, the huge stone was rolled away, and Jesus walked out of his borrowed tomb. When the women went to the garden early Sunday morning, they were shocked by what they saw.

"Who took his body away, and where did they take it?" they wondered.

Seven times the Gospels record Jesus telling them he would rise from the dead. The disciples didn't understand what he meant, and neither did the ladies who visited the tomb. When they saw the empty tomb, they didn't think he was alive. But he was, and he is today. Jesus Christ was raised from the dead, and he lives forevermore. This is the good-news story.

Have you come to know this story?

I don't mean as a historical fact. Has your dark, hopeless Friday come to an end—the searching, the restlessness, the emptiness, the guilt and shame? Have you found what you were looking for in the person of Jesus Christ? Has he given you new life?

If so, the resurrection story has become your story. Sunday is here for you. As John wrote in his Gospel account, "Very truly I tell you, the one who believes has everlasting life" (John 6:47).

You have everlasting life. Let that soak in.

Like Jesus, you've walked out of your spiritual tomb fully alive—raised to walk in the newness of life here and now. Sunday has arrived for you, but not for the world. It's still Friday for this world of darkness.

This raises a very important question: How do you live a Sunday life in a Friday world?

In the World

You may have heard this popular saying in Christian circles: "We are in the world but not of the world." This saying isn't in the Bible, but it does summarize what the Bible says on the subject. The idea is a central theme that runs through Jesus's high-priestly prayer for his disciples recorded in John 17.

> I will remain in the world no longer, but they are still in the world, and I am coming to you. Holy Father, protect them by the power of your name, the name you gave me, so that they may be one as we are one...
>
> I have given them your word and the world has hated them, for they are not of the world any more than I am of the world. My prayer is not that you take them out of the world but that you protect them from the evil one. They are not of the world, even as I am not of it. Sanctify them by the truth; your word is truth (verses 11,14-17).

Yes, we live in this world, but we are not of it. We do not belong. We are, as Peter wrote, "foreigners and exiles" (1 Peter 2:11), or "aliens and strangers" (NASB). We do not fit in anymore.

When the Bible speaks of the world, it is not referring to planet Earth. Earth and all of God's creation will be restored. There will be a new heaven and a new earth. Right now creation waits to be freed from the curse that resulted from Adam and Eve's sin. Paul brought out this point in his letter to the Romans.

> The creation was subjected to frustration, not by its own choice, but by the will of the one who subjected it, in hope that the creation itself will be liberated from its bondage to decay and brought into the freedom and glory of the children of God (Romans 8:20-21).

Sometimes, this truth escapes us. God is going to free creation from its bondage in the same way he freed us from our bondage to sin and death. Jesus's death, burial, and resurrection guarantee the fulfillment of this part of God's plan. It will happen when we, the sons of God, are revealed.

"The world" refers to the world system. It consists of "the lust of the flesh, the lust of the eyes, and the pride of life" (1 John 2:16).

These things do not come from God, and they will pass away. Only those who do the will of God will live forever. Doing the will of God—this is the key to living a Sunday life in a Friday world. For now, we live this new way of life surrounded by the world system.

This world system had its genesis at the tree of the knowledge of good and evil. All the elements became fully operational. Eve wanted to be like God—the lust of the flesh. She saw that the fruit of the tree was pleasing to the eye—the lust of the eyes. And it was desirable for gaining wisdom—the pride of life. Mankind has been feeding on that tree ever since. The system is built on unbelief. It is expressed through the deeds of darkness.

Some of these deeds can look good on the surface. For example, the Pharisees prayed in public. Prayer is good, and the Bible encourages us to pray. For them, however, prayer was nothing more than an empty, dead work. Their prayers were motivated by the wisdom they gained from the tree of the knowledge of good and evil. Jesus warned against this type of praying. "When you pray, do not be like the hypocrites, for they love to pray standing in the synagogues and on the street corners to be seen by others. Truly I tell you, they have received their reward in full" (Matthew 6:5).

These hypocrites were operating from a heart of unbelief. From that heart, they reinterpreted the law, the Mosaic covenant, to establish their own standard for righteousness. They took what was holy, righteous, and good and molded it to fit with the world system. Paul was one of those guys. He boasted of being faultless as to legalistic righteousness. But after meeting Jesus, he clearly saw that this wasn't the righteousness of God. He describes the Israelites' misguided efforts.

> Since they did not know the righteousness of God and sought to establish their own, they did not submit to

God's righteousness. Christ is the culmination of the law so that there may be righteousness for everyone who believes (Romans 10:3-4).

Here, Paul draws the line between the way of the world and the way of Christ. It is the difference between law and grace. Resurrection life is lived by grace through faith.

The Real Reason

In February 2013, my mom had a major medical scare. Shortness of breath and overall fatigue landed her in an emergency room one evening. Now, Mom is not quick to run to a doctor at the first sign of an ache or pain. She doesn't even like to take aspirin. But she knew she needed to be in that emergency room.

The physician on call wasn't sure what was going on inside Mom, but she knew it was something serious. She checked Mom into the hospital and scheduled a cardio angiogram for early the next morning. My sister Gina called me to let me know the situation.

The next day, I was playing golf with friends of the ministry from California. I hit my tee ball on the eleventh hole and started my walk down the fairway. My phone rang. It was my sister Lisa. The angiogram showed a total blockage around Mom's heart. As soon as the radiologist saw it, he knew she needed surgery immediately. They rushed her to the operating room to perform emergency bypass surgery.

I was undone. I left the golf course and headed straight to the airport. When I arrived at the hospital, the surgery was complete, and Mom was resting in her room. The surgery was successful, and she has since recovered nicely. That never would have happened apart from the angiogram. That X-ray helped her team of doctors diagnose her problem, which led them to the solution.

The angiogram wasn't the solution. It was powerless to do anything at all to repair Mom's heart. She needed the skilled hands of her surgeon to fix the problem.

I share this story because it illustrates the nature and purpose of the law. Its purpose is much like the purpose of an angiogram. The law diagnoses our spiritual problem, but it cannot provide the cure. Read what Paul had to say about the law: "No one will be declared righteous in God's sight by the works of the law; rather, through the law we become conscious of sin" (Romans 3:20).

What does the law show us? Our sin. This is what God designed it to do. It is a spiritual tool in his hands to draw our attention toward Jesus Christ. The law can't save us. That is Jesus's job. The law points us to him. Here is the purpose of the law in crystal clear language: "The law was our guardian until Christ came that we might be justified by faith. Now that this faith has come, we are no longer under a guardian" (Galatians 3:24-25).

Discerning the purpose of the law was a big issue in the early church. It's still a big issue. Some first-century believers, particularly the group gathered in Galatia, struggled to understand the purpose of the law. They looked at it as the means of living the Christian life and embraced it as their rule of life. Paul didn't bother being delicate when he addressed the situation: "You foolish Galatians..." Ouch! That's not very nice, but I imagine it got their attention.

He asked them, "I would like to learn just one thing from you: Did you receive the Spirit by the works of the law, or by believing what you heard? Are you so foolish? After beginning by means of the Spirit, are you now trying to finish by means of the flesh?" (Galatians 3:2-3). They went back to the tree of the knowledge of good and evil. They leaned on their own understanding to determine the purpose of the law. They missed it.

Here is what we need to know. Law, as a rule of life, rests squarely on the shoulders of human effort. But human effort doesn't cut it when it comes to living in the newness of life. A quick read through the letter of Galatians shows that the believers relying on human effort were...

> deserting the one who called them (1:6)
> turning to a different gospel (1:6)
> being confused (1:7)
> trying to please men (1:10)
> fearful of others (2:12)
> dividing the body of Christ (2:12)
> hypocritical (2:13)
> not acting in line with the truth of the gospel (2:14)
> setting aside the grace of God (2:21)
> turning back to weak and miserable forces (4:9)
> letting themselves be burdened by a yoke of slavery (5:1)
> using their freedom to indulge the flesh (5:13)
> backbiting and devouring one another (5:15)

Human effort didn't work out so well for the Galatians. It doesn't work for us either. To be clear, Paul is talking about applying human effort to the fulfillment of the law—the Ten Commandments and the entire Mosaic covenant—in order to become righteous. Human effort applied to any set of rules or regulations produces the same harmful results.

The reason God gave the law was to show you your need for Jesus, to help you diagnose your problem. Now that you are alive in Christ, you are no longer under the supervision of the law. Just as the law had a purpose for the nation of Israel, it had a purpose for you. But that purpose does not supersede God's greater purpose for you in Christ. Paul put it this way: "The law, introduced 430 years later, does not set aside the covenant previously established by God and thus do away with the promise" (Galatians 3:17).

Remember the number 430 from chapter 11? Here is its significance. God in his grace made a promise to Abraham to bless the world through his offspring. That offspring is Jesus. This has always been God's plan. The law didn't change that plan at all. It simply served the greater purpose of God's promise. In addition, the Mosaic covenant was a temporary covenant. It was time-stamped to end when Christ appeared. When Jesus arrived on the scene of your life, the purpose of the law was fulfilled in you. That law has given way to the life of Jesus Christ in you. You are connected to him.

The first step in living a Sunday life in a Friday world is to let go of human effort.

You've already been released from the law. It has done its work in you. As a result, you "died to the law through the body of Christ, that you might belong to another... [Now you] serve in the new way of the Spirit, and not in the old way of the written code" (Romans 7:4,6).

That new way of life is a life of faith. It is a life that is led by and empowered by the Spirit of God.

By the Spirit

"So I say, walk by the Spirit, and you will not gratify the desires of the flesh" (Galatians 5:16). To live by the Spirit is to live by the love of God. The Spirit pours the love of God into your heart (Romans 5:5). He strengthens you in your inner being with the power to grasp how high, how deep, how long, and how wide the love of God is (Ephesians 3:16-19). He compels you to express his love to others. This is the Sunday life. As Paul said, this is what counts—"faith expressing itself through love" (Galatians 5:6).

Living by the Spirit frees you from gratifying the desires of the flesh. It is important to understand this distinction. So many well-intentioned believers spend a lifetime trying to overcome sin in their lives. They wake up each morning with this prayer on their lips: "Lord, please help me not sin today." At the end of the day, they look back only to see their prayer went unanswered. They have their focus in the wrong place. Here is a more meaningful and practical prayer: "Lord, teach me to abide in you and to follow the leading of your Spirit in my life."

You can count on this—God's Spirit will never lead you into sin. He leads you into all truth. He leads you down the paths of righteousness. He leads you to love and serve others. This life of faith is simply ordering everything that you are and do around the work of God's Spirit in your life. Peter put it this way:

> His divine power has given us everything we need for a godly life through our knowledge of him who called us by his own glory and goodness. Through these he has given us his very great and precious promises, so that through them you may participate in the divine nature, having escaped the corruption in the world caused by evil desires (2 Peter 1:3-4).

Living by the Spirit is trusting God to complete the work he began in you. You can count on him to complete this task even though you don't always cooperate.

The modern GPS navigational system illustrates the Holy Spirit's work in our lives. Here's how it works. The unit receives signals from 24 satellites orbiting earth and locates your position. You type in a destination, and the unit then maps out the best route to get you from your starting point to your ending point. Along the way, you hear step-by-step voice directions until you reach your final destination.

The voice for my system is female. I affectionately call her Mildred. She gets me where I need to go. The feature I like the most is the system's ability to recalculate directions when I make a wrong turn or take the wrong exit off a highway.

Mildred doesn't condemn me for not following her directions. She doesn't call me stupid or berate me for making a mistake. She simply recalculates and gives me a new route to get me to my destination. This is what the Holy Spirit does in our lives. He charts a course to get us to our destination, a destination spelled out for us in Romans 8:29: "Those God foreknew he also predestined to be conformed to the image of his Son."

Even though we know the destination, we are not capable of mapping out a course to get ourselves there. The Spirit guides us on this new journey. As we abide in him and trust in him, he directs our paths. And we find him at every turn telling us which way to go.

When we do get off course (and we will), the Holy Spirit faithfully recalculates our journey and continues his work of conforming us to the image of his Son. He does so without condemnation. He doesn't manipulate us with fear and guilt. He uses our mistakes, reminding us of the forgiveness we have in Christ, and works them together for our good. He comforts our hearts with this amazing promise: "He who began a good work in you will carry it on to completion until the day of Christ Jesus" (Philippians 1:6).

You are not alone on your journey. God is with you every step of the way. His Spirit will get you to your destination. Trust him, rely on him, and live out what he is working in your life. Paul summed it up best.

My dear friends, as you have always obeyed—not only in my presence, but now much more in my absence—continue to work out your salvation with fear and trembling, for it is God who works in you to will and to act according to his good purpose (Philippians 2:12-13).

That's Sunday living in a Friday world.

14

The Goal

My mom once worked for a time-management company. This company sold day planners and organizers based on the time-management system it had designed. They primarily sold to businesses to help employees be more productive in the workplace. Mom's company also trained employees to use the system.

Setting goals and objectives were key ingredients to the system's success. You start with the end in mind. This is the place where a project or task finds its completion. Then you outline the steps you'll take to get there, assigning each step a due date. The system worked for many, many people. You may be using something similar today to help you accomplish your goals in life.

My mom worked for this company about the same time that I began to discover the grace of God. Mom gave me an organizer. When I tried to use it back then, it always made me think about

God's goals. I wondered what his goals were for my life. In other words, I wanted to know God's will. I am sure this has crossed your mind a time or two as well.

Knowing God's will is one of our deepest desires, yet it can be one of our most frustrating quests.

When you hear or read the phrase "God's will," what comes to mind? Most would frame their answer in terms of God's plan for them. They want to know how to choose whom to marry, where to live, and what to do in life. For example, Steve called our radio program to discuss a big decision he was facing. He had two job opportunities and didn't know which one to take. He explained the situation and then asked, "What is God's will for me?"

Steve did not want to make the wrong decision. He was stuck in the mud. He was so afraid he might miss God's perfect will and what that might mean for the future. I can tell you, being stuck in the mud like Steve is not God's will. God has called us to a life of freedom that is built on the foundation of God's promise in Romans 8:28: "We know that in all things God works for the good of those who love him, who have been called according to his purpose." This is a win-win proposition. But to get there, we need to shift our thinking regarding God's will.

The Shift

Instead of thinking of God's will in terms of a plan, let's shift gears and look at it in terms of a legal will.

Legally, a will is a statement of a person's wishes concerning the disposal of his property after death. When my dad died, everything he owned passed to Mom. That was his desire, and he explicitly expressed it in his will.

God has a will like that. It's called the new covenant. In this will, God expressed his desires for you and me. The original document appeared first in the book of Jeremiah. God chose to announce the specifics of this will through this prophet some 600 years before the time of Jesus. God was expressing at that time what he had in mind for us all along. It was an announcement of what was to come.

Before it could take effect, the one who made it had to die. "In the case of a will, it is necessary to prove the death of the one who made it, because a will is in force only when somebody has died; it never takes effect while the one who made it is living" (Hebrews 9:16-17).

When Jesus gathered his disciples for the last supper, he raised a cup and said, "This cup is the new covenant in my blood, which is poured out for you" (Luke 22:20). More than 600 years had passed since it was first mentioned. As if out of nowhere, Jesus tells them the time has come for the new covenant to be fulfilled. His shed blood would make it so.

The next day, Jesus died. He cried out in victory, "It is finished." The old had gone, the new had come. The long-awaited new covenant was now in full force. When did the new covenant begin? At the cross. Jesus's death changed everything.

This new covenant is a covenant of grace. It is not like the old covenant, which was more like a contract between two parties. It was an "if...then" covenant. It included conditions for its fulfillment, but there are no conditions in the new covenant. God promises, God fulfills. In this new covenant, we see God's unmerited favor in full display—the free gift of grace.

I've already mentioned several promises included in the new covenant. Now let's look at it in its entirety. As wills go, it's not very long—only four provisions.

> This is the covenant I will establish with the people of Israel
> after that time, declares the Lord.

> I will put my laws in their minds
>   and write them on their hearts.
> I will be their God,
>   and they will be my people.
> No longer will they teach their neighbor,
>   or say to one another, "Know the Lord,"
> because they will all know me,
>   from the least of them to the greatest.
> For I will forgive their wickedness
>   and will remember their sins no more (Hebrews 8:10-12).

Don't underestimate the far reach of these promises where your life in Christ is concerned. These contain everything you need for life and godliness. In this new covenant, you can live life to the full, which is God's will for you. He has rescued you through Christ and delivered you to this end.

Be Perfect

I've taught and attended small-group Bible studies in about every type of venue possible. The latest meets in the card room at a local country club. One study I attended was held at the Telos Fitness Center in north Dallas. I mention this simply because the name is intriguing.

Telos is a Greek word that has philosophical roots extending back to Plato and Aristotle. The word refers to an end or a purpose. Plato and Aristotle believed that there were ends or purposes to which all of life was leading. In other words, what happens in the world isn't accidental. There is a propelling force moving the world to a stated end.

Telos also has biblical roots. Along with its cognates, it is used often in the New Testament and is significant in telling the gospel story.

The first time we see this word in the New Testament is in Matthew 5:48. It occurs in the middle of Jesus's Sermon on the Mount in an extremely troubling statement: "Be perfect, therefore, as your heavenly Father is perfect." This statement is troubling because we equate perfection with being flawless or not having any defects. We know we can't be perfect by this standard. If you think otherwise, I encourage you to reread Jesus's sermon. He made it perfectly clear that flawless perfection is beyond your reach.

You may have avoided adultery and murder, but have you lived free of lust or anger?

Jesus isn't concerned merely with the letter of the law. He opened the hood and showed us the spirit of the law. At that point, we miss the mark and miss it badly.

Perhaps Jesus had something else in mind. Maybe the point is that Jesus wants us to find completeness in him. One of the definitions for "perfect"—*teleios*—is "wanting for nothing." Perfection in this sense is a place of contentment. That is God's ultimate aim for us—that we find contentment in him. Adam and Eve were perfectly content in the Garden. They were living out their God-given purpose. They were reflecting to the world the image of their Creator. But then sin entered the picture and knocked them off course. And it knocked us off course as well. It grabbed the chains of control and forced us down another path.

When we are in sin's grip, we can't do anything to get back on course. Not even the law can deliver us to this end. This is a hard lesson for us to learn. You cannot achieve God's purpose for your life through obedience to the law. It is impossible. The writer of Hebrews was very clear on this point.

> If perfection could have been attained through the Levitical priesthood—and indeed the law given to the people

established that priesthood—why was there still need for another priest to come, one in the order of Melchizedek, not in the order of Aaron?…

The former regulation is set aside because it was weak and useless (for the law made nothing perfect), and a better hope is introduced, by which we draw near to God (7:11,18-19).

The law will not take you to God's intended goal for you. If you try to use it that way, you'll find it to be weak and useless. The law does not have sufficient strength or power to make you perfect. It cannot break sin's control in your life.

The fault isn't in the law. The blame falls squarely on us. I wanted to be God's guy. That was my end goal. Law and self-effort were my means of accomplishing that end. But I found out that I was weak and useless—ouch! That lesson was painful but true. I could not free myself from sin's control. As a matter of fact, the harder I tried, the tighter sin's grip became.

All along that path, the law judged me, condemned me, and showed me that sin's goal for me was death. That's what it was designed to do. Paul called it the ministry of death and the ministry of condemnation.

The law can't deliver us to the goal. Only grace can do that. What the law was powerless to do, Christ did.

Look at what Christ accomplished for you. Hebrews 10:10 says that you have been made holy through the sacrifice of Jesus Christ once for all. Hebrews 10:14 says that by that one sacrifice he made you perfect forever. Jesus cleansed you, made you holy, and then delivered you smack-dab in the center of God's will, right where you belong. Paul put it this way:

Since we have been justified through faith, we have peace with God through our Lord Jesus Christ, through whom we have gained access by faith into this grace in which we now stand. And we boast in the hope of the glory of God (Romans 5:1-2).

A Declaration

Do you know the story of the Marshall Thundering Herd football program? On November 14, 1970, the team boarded Southern Airways flight 932 in Kinston, North Carolina, after a tough loss at the hands of the East Carolina Pirates. At 7:36 that evening, as the plane was descending through the fog and rain, it collided with the tops of trees and then crashed into the side of a hill just short of the Huntington airport. All 75 people on board were killed.

The Marshall football program was wiped out that day. The tragedy left many wondering if Marshall would ever field a football team again.

Marshall was determined to come back. The university hired Jack Lengyel as the new head coach to resurrect the program. No one was sure if he (or anyone else) could do it.

Finding players was one of his toughest tasks. He recruited players from the baseball and basketball teams, and he opened the doors to walk-ons. The first season after the crash, Marshall won one game, a come-from-behind thriller against Xavier.

Lengyel had done his job. He breathed new life into the Marshall football program.

In 2006, Hollywood told the story on-screen in *We Are Marshall*. Matthew McConaughey played Jack Lengyel. It is one of my favorite sports movies. The story is deeply moving and inspirational. In one of the scenes, the board of regents is deliberating the future of the program. Students gather outside the building and begin to chant, "We are Marshall!" This was the turning point. It galvanized the university, the students, and the community in support of the program. I'll admit, the movie really tugged at my heartstrings because of the connection I saw with the new-covenant life we've been called to live.

"We are Marshall" was much more than a chant. It was a bold declaration of purpose. The football program was here to stay, and there was no turning back.

Are you ready to make a declaration? God in his grace and mercy delivered you into the new covenant. That is where he wants you to be, and that's where you are. Think about this: You will never be outside God's favor. You are in his favor, and there is no turning back. It's time to fully embrace who you are.

I've told this story at conferences on several occasions. At the end, I ask the crowd to stand and declare, "We are new covenant." Today I am asking you to make that same declaration. It's time to fully embrace God's perfect plan and will for you. It's time to say, "I am a new-covenant believer."

If you need encouragement, follow Paul's lead. "He has made us competent as ministers of a new covenant—not of the letter but of the Spirit; for the letter kills, but the Spirit gives life" (2 Corinthians 3:6).

The Work of Grace

Grace is powerful and active. It is not passive or reactive in the least. Grace is proactive.

Grace is Jesus Christ living his life in you. As someone once said, Jesus Christ has been raised from the dead, and he is on the loose. He is on the loose in you.

Jesus is the pioneer and perfecter of faith (Hebrews 12:2). When you heard the message, Jesus pioneered faith in you. And now by grace he is perfecting that faith, bringing it to maturity.

This is another variation of the word *telos*.

Before we continue down this road, let's stop and see where we've been. Jesus taught that we should be perfect, as our Father in heaven is perfect. That's the goal. We've learned that human effort is not enough and that the law is powerless to deliver us to this end. Jesus's mission through his death, burial, and resurrection—God's grace in action—rescued us from the realm of darkness and delivered us into the kingdom of God. By Christ's completed work ("it is finished" is another variation of the word *telos*), we've been made perfect forever. We are exactly where God wants us to be.

The work of grace does not stop there, however. Jesus is fully focused on perfecting our faith and, as we have seen in previous chapters, completing the work that he began (Philippians 1:6).

Read through the letters of the New Testament, and you will see this process taking place through the trials of life. Life on planet Earth is filled with trials and tribulations. They are constantly coming at us like waves to the shore. As Jesus said: "In this world you will have trouble" (John 16:33).

Even so, we can take heart. Jesus has overcome the world. Jesus is now living in us, and he teaches us how to abide in him through the trials and tribulations of life. He is perfecting our faith.

James, Jesus's half-brother, knew about trials and tribulations. As the leader of the church in Jerusalem, he faced opposition from both the Romans and the Jews. Out of that experience, he wrote, "Consider it pure joy, my brothers and sisters, whenever you face trials of many kinds" (James 1:2).

Each trial raises the question, is Jesus enough? We're not always sure, are we? Sometimes we doubt and even worry that he will not be enough. Time and time again, Jesus proves he is. And each time he does, he moves our faith down the road to completion, as James discovered. "You know that the testing of your faith produces perseverance. Let perseverance finish its work so that you may be mature and complete, not lacking anything" (verses 3-4).

For Paul, the maturing of his faith led to a hope that did not disappoint because God had poured his love into Paul's heart by the Holy Spirit (Romans 5:3-5). No wonder he wrote that nothing can separate us from the love of God (Romans 8:38-39).

Through all that Peter endured, Jesus proved to him that his faith was genuine. Peter's belief in Christ filled him with an "inexpressible and glorious joy," and he received the goal of his faith, the salvation of his soul (1 Peter 1:6-9). The writer of Hebrews weighed in as well. He said we should endure hardship as discipline. The end result is a harvest of righteousness and peace for those trained by it (Hebrews 12:7-11).

Jesus is enough. His grace is sufficient.

When Paul was struggling with his thorn in the flesh, he prayed three times that God would remove it. God did not remove the thorn. He had another answer in mind. Paul wrote, "But he said to me, 'My grace is sufficient for you, for my power is made perfect in weakness'" (2 Corinthians 12:9). Jesus was bringing Paul's faith to maturity, moving it toward completion, taking Paul to the place where his soul was fully satisfied in God.

The Lord told Paul not only that his grace was sufficient but that his power is made perfect in weakness. Made perfect—there's our word again. Jesus's power finds its full strength in us when we are most dependent on him. That's when we recognize that apart from Christ we can do nothing that leads us to our goal—fully abiding in him and experiencing the full measure of his resurrected life. *That* is new-covenant living.

Sometimes we try to take the bull by the horns. "I've got this, Lord." Although we don't say it out loud, we sometimes believe we are sufficient for the task. We know what to do to produce the desired outcome. I think the Bible calls that leaning on our own understanding. I fell into that trap several years ago. It was one of the most difficult situations in my life. I desperately wanted love to win out. I put my nose to the task of making it happen. All of my efforts and the extreme stress of the situation landed me in a hospital.

I left work one afternoon not feeling well. When I got home, Jeanna knew something was terribly wrong. She monitored my blood pressure for about an hour. It kept going up, and it finally reached a point where something had to happen. She took me to a nearby urgent care center. They took my blood pressure and then told Jeanna to get me to an emergency room as quickly as possible.

A nurse immediately called us into an examination room. At that point my blood pressure was off the charts. I was in trouble. The nurses were focused and moved quickly to stabilize me. They wheeled me to a back room and put an oxygen mask on me. At that moment, I felt safe, as if Jesus were saying to me, "My grace is sufficient." I stayed in the hospital overnight and was released the next day. I left the hospital realizing my self-effort had done nothing but internalize the trouble. When I let go and relied on Jesus, I could see him at work and could trust him to work the situation for good.

Jesus is enough. He is more than adequate for any circumstance or problem. We can cast our cares on him, for he truly cares for us. That's what Paul did.

> I will boast all the more gladly about my weaknesses,
> so that Christ's power may rest on me. That is why, for

Christ's sake, I delight in weaknesses, in insults, in hardships, in persecutions, in difficulties. For when I am
weak, then I am strong (2 Corinthians 12:9-10).

You are perfect in Christ. You are a new-covenant believer. His
grace is sufficient to bring your faith to maturity. Keep your eyes
on him.

15

Eternal Life

Do you remember your first day of school? I don't have any real recollection of that day at all. I do know my first day of school was at Waterman Street Elementary in Marietta, Georgia. My teacher was Mrs. Paste. I don't remember what I wore that day, who I sat by, or what happened. My mom, however, vividly remembers one thing that happened. She later related that story to me.

Mrs. Paste wanted to know something about each student and their families. She asked us to answer this question: What does your dad do?

When it was my turn, I stood and said, "My dad sleeps all day."

My answer raised Mrs. Paste's eyebrows. It must have concerned her that I thought that my dad did nothing but sleep all day. She talked to Mom to find out the real story. Mom couldn't believe what

I said, and it infuriated her. She still gets a twinge inside when she thinks back to my response to that question.

Back then, my dad was completing his college degree and working three jobs to support the family. Every chance he got, he tried to catch up on his sleep. As a five-year-old, I wasn't aware of his heavy schedule and all of his responsibilities. I was just a kid. Seeing him asleep during the day is the one thing that came to mind when Mrs. Paste posed her question.

Like any five-year-old, I really didn't know my dad. I knew I belonged to him. I was his son and he was my father. But that was about the extent of my relationship with him. I didn't know him beyond that. I didn't know what he was really like or what made him tick.

That changed as I grew older. I began to find out more and more about this man I called Dad. I found out that he loved sports, especially basketball. That he hated iced tea, peanut butter, and the song "The Twelve Days of Christmas." That he wanted to learn how to swim (he finally did when he was in his sixties). That he loved Mom more than any other person on the planet. That he once wanted to go to seminary. That he was honest, hardworking, and loyal. That family was important. That he was proud of me and my sisters and would do anything for us. That he knew a lot about math. That he could laugh uncontrollably when watching slapstick comedy. That he loved Jesus Christ.

Life is about relationships. Knowing and being known. I was privileged to know my dad. As I grew older, people told me I was a lot like him. I can think of no better compliment. Through our relationship, I learned more and more about him, and he rubbed off on me. His values became my values. Watching him, I learned the importance of responsibility, telling the truth, and sticking to your convictions.

Concerning his convictions, one story stands out. Mom and Dad never had alcohol in the house. They never made a big deal about it—it just wasn't something they did. Once, on a camping trip in Florida, a gentleman in the neighboring campsite offered Dad a beer. My ears perked up. I wanted to know if Dad would take the beer. In a nonchalant way, he looked at the gentleman and said, "Thanks for the offer, but no thank you." The two of them carried on with their conversation. I was impressed, and I've never forgotten that moment.

As a husband, he put real flesh and blood to the command to love Mom as Christ loved the church. She was the most important person in the world to him. It's not that they never fought or disagreed or got out of sorts. They did, but it never lasted long. When Dad died, there were no regrets. Nothing was left unsaid. Nothing was left undone. Mom knew she had been truly and genuinely loved. I want Jeanna to feel the same way.

I also knew that he believed in me and trusted Christ's work in my life. The day I moved to Dallas, he put my face in his hands and prayed for me. It was a father blessing his son. His words were simple, but they imparted courage and hope and assurance. When I left, I cried the first 600 miles of the drive to Texas.

I admire my dad more than any other man. Every time I think about him, I thank God for his life and for the pleasure of calling him my dad. I also think about a verse in the Bible that has become my favorite. In my mind, all roads in the Bible lead to John 17:3: "Now this is eternal life: that they know you, the only true God, and Jesus Christ, whom you have sent."

This is the only verse in the Bible that defines eternal life. Jesus defined it in terms of relationship. We Christians are quick to point out that Christianity is not a religion; it is a relationship. That's true, but it is so much more. This relationship, our knowing God the Father and Jesus Christ, constitutes eternal life. It is a "by grace through faith" relationship, a spiritual union that conforms us to the likeness of Jesus. In other words, through this relationship, God rubs off on us, and we become like him. The Bible gives this stunning compliment to those who are called children of God: "In this world we are like Jesus" (1 John 4:17).

As we learned in the previous chapter, knowing God personally and intimately is one of the promises of the new covenant. Let me share the promise with you again: "No longer will they teach their neighbor, or say to one another, 'Know the Lord,' because they will all know me, from the least of them to the greatest" (Hebrews 8:11). Dan DeHaan, the teacher God used to open my eyes to the grace of God, wrote, "God created men to know Him. God created men to enjoy Him."[1]

God took away your sins, reconciled you to himself, justified you, sanctified you, made you alive, and poured his Spirit into your life for this single purpose. The great story of the gospel is that you've been raised to walk in the newness of life. You have been raised to know and enjoy him. This is ultimate freedom. This is eternal life.

The Relationship

Why did Jesus come to earth? There are several different biblical answers to this question. I like the answer John gave early in his Gospel account: "No one has ever seen God, but the one and only Son, who is himself God and is in closest relationship with the Father, has made him known" (John 1:18).

Through his life, Jesus showed us the Father. To his disciples, he said, "Anyone who has seen me has seen the Father" (John 14:9). We can discern some of God's attributes through creation, such as his eternal power and divine nature. These are plain for everyone to see.

We can also see God's wrath against all godlessness, as Paul wrote in Romans 1. Beyond these traits, the nature of God is veiled, so much so that the philosophers in Athens inscribed these words on an altar: "To an unknown God" (Acts 17:23). Only in Jesus is God the Father made known to man.

Some would rather keep God unknown. They fear finding out what he thinks about them. They don't want to know the truth. And so they come up with their own ideas as to what God is like. Talk about a distorted view.

Apart from Jesus, we make God out to look like a Picasso painting. It's our inherent fear that paints such a distorted view. We think of him as a mean, judgmental, and angry being who can never be pleased. Let me ask you. Before you heard the gospel and responded in faith, what did you think about God? How did you describe him? What did you suppose he thought about you?

How would you answer those three questions now that Jesus has revealed the Father to you? Hopefully, you see a stark contrast between your earlier guesses and your current perspective. The difference is that now you are seeing him through the person and work of Jesus Christ.

Let's take a look to see how this relationship evolves. Genesis 1:1 is the best place to start. "In the beginning, God..." He initiated the whole thing. He reached down to you through Jesus Christ. That's grace. His grace worked in you a desire to know him. That's faith. At God's initiative, a union was formed—you in Christ and Christ in you. His Spirit was joined to your human spirit, and the two were fused together. That was the point when eternal life began for you, the point when you started learning the truth about the God of the universe. In his love and grace, God started making himself known to you in a real and personal way.

Children, Young Men, and Fathers

God is an infinite being. We are finite. He reveals himself to us more and more as we are ready to receive. Jesus made this point to the disciples: "I have much more to say to you, more than you can now bear" (John 16:12). Our knowledge of him grows over time. The word "know" conveys a continuous process. Our initial, incomplete knowledge grows into a fuller or more complete knowledge. I like the way John sketched out this progression in his first letter. He described how our knowledge of the Lord grows by addressing three different groups—children, young men, and fathers.

He was very direct in his letter to each of these groups. To the children, John said, "Your sins are forgiven on account of his name," and "You know the Father" (1 John 2:12,14). What do these statements tell you about the character of God and his desire for you? They tell me that God wants to be with me and that he wants me to be with him. Did you know that about God when you were lost? I didn't. I thought he was disgusted and wanted nothing to do with me. Forgiveness tells another story. Through forgiveness, God opened our eyes to recognize him as Father, and he sent his Spirit into our hearts, by which we cry out, "*Abba*, Father" (Galatians 4:6).

If you are a new believer, let God implant these two truths deeply in your heart. Your sins are forgiven, and you are a child of God. You belong. You are in the family.

To the young men, John wrote, "You have overcome the evil one," and "You are strong, and the word of God lives in you" (1 John 2:13-14). Young men have a deeper knowledge of Jesus Christ than do little children. Their knowledge is built on what God revealed to them as children. The truth of God's love and grace lives in them and empowers them to stand strong in the Lord against the fiery darts of the enemy. This truth sets them apart from the world and enables them to live as children of light in this world of darkness.

To the fathers, John wrote, "You know him who is from the beginning" (1 John 2:13). For emphasis, John repeated this statement. What he means by this is that the fathers' knowledge of God is reaching fullness. God has fully aligned the hearts of these fathers with his. They know what God is about in this world and what his purposes are. They know, as N.T. Wright so clearly stated, that "salvation is not simply God's gift to his people but God's gift through his people."[2] God's love for the world has become theirs.

This brings us full circle. In the first chapter, I defined grace. Here we see its ultimate purpose—to connect us to the love of God. With every stage in this progression, our knowledge of God's love grows and expands. Jesus Christ makes the love of God known to us. He places on our eyes a lens of grace that brings the truth that God is love into clear focus.

A New Command

This understanding of the grace of God is not without its critics. This doesn't make sense to me. How could any believer in Christ be critical of grace saving them and now sustaining them? Yet many are critical. They drone away about taking grace too far and using it as a license to sin. They say grace needs to be balanced by law. That is not God's plan. God's plan is "by grace through faith." This is the balance God strikes in us.

These critics also complain that this emphasis on grace, which some call hyper-grace, removes all law from our lives. The theological word is "antinomianism." It means "without law." However, this criticism does not hold up under the scrutiny of the Word.

As believers, we live in the new covenant. This new covenant is our rule of life, and it is a covenant of grace. The first provision is that God writes his laws on our hearts and places them in our minds. This is not the law of Moses, or the old covenant. It's the law of faith (Romans 3:27), the law of hope (1 Peter 1:3), and the law of love (1 John 3:23). As new-covenant believers, we are not without law. The writer of Hebrews stated, "When the priesthood is changed, the law must be changed also" (Hebrews 7:12). The priesthood changed. Jesus is now the high priest, and we have become the royal priest-hood. As a result, the law changed. Our new way is by the law of the Spirit of life (Romans 8:2), the law of Christ (Galatians 6:2), and the law of liberty (James 1:25).

This new life, this new way, this new covenant is written by "the Spirit of the living God, not on tablets of stone but on tablets of human hearts" (2 Corinthians 3:3). Grace does not leave us with-out law. Nor are we left to carry these laws out through human effort. God's Spirit works in us. He animates our faith, anchors our hope, and sources our love. He has lifted us out of that old way and ordered our steps to walk in the way of love. And all this ties back to Jesus's definition of eternal life.

I'll let the apostle John connect the dots: "Dear friends, let us love one another, for love comes from God. Everyone who loves has been born of God and knows God. Whoever does not love does not know God, because God is love" (1 John 4:7-8). Loving others means you have been born of God and you know God. Knowing God and Jesus Christ is eternal life. To know God is to know that he is love. This is the mark that distinguishes us from the world and is the evidence we are the disciples of Jesus Christ (John 13:34-35).

The world does not know God. That's the problem. Tragically, it is also a problem in the church.

Many describe the church today as anemic. Its influence in the culture is waning. Its own morals are decaying. It seems to be losing ground at every turn. What's the problem? That's the great dilemma of the day. It has left many church leaders scratching their heads in frustration and grasping at straws to fix the problem. We've tried to regain our clout through politics. We've added the flavor of relevance to the message to make it palatable. We've moved from traditional to contemporary services. We've used the power of celebrity to harness attention.

Maybe the problem is that we've lost our first love. Maybe we've lost sight of the goal of the good news. Maybe we've become so enamored with the gifts of grace that we've missed the Giver. Maybe we've lost sight of our greatest asset.

We have been entrusted with the knowledge of God. That's what distinguishes us from the world. That's the story of the gospel.

True Freedom

True freedom allows us to know and to be known. It also enables us to be generous and to look toward the needs of others. This is the idea behind Paul's warning, "You, my brothers and sisters, were called to be free. But do not use your freedom to indulge the flesh; rather, serve one another humbly in love" (Galatians 5:13).

Consider the apostle Peter. He denied the Lord three times. After he did, he wept bitterly. In his mind, he had disappointed Jesus and let him down. He feared the worst—that the Lord would reject him. He learned something different after the resurrection. Jesus restored him by showing him the full extent of his love. He lifted Peter out of his despair and counted him worthy to feed his sheep. That's grace.

This deep connection to the love of Christ compelled Peter to march from Joppa to Caesarea to meet with Cornelius and his household. Cornelius was a Gentile. Entering his house was a violation of Jewish law, but Peter entered anyway. God was at work in Peter's heart, moving him to feed God's sheep. Peter was willing to defile himself according to the traditions of the law because he had just learned something about the heart of God. He had learned that God is not partial, that his love and life are available to all.

Peter opened his mouth and told this Gentile family about God's purpose for them in Christ. And they opened their hearts and received the gift of life. Peter knew the Lord. This heart knowledge changed and transformed him, and others responded to his unwavering message.

The gift of grace is Jesus Christ. You have the joy and privilege of knowing him and walking in his love. You have the privilege of making him known in this world of darkness. As Paul said, through your knowledge of Christ, you "shine among them like stars in the sky as you hold firmly to the word of life" (Philippians 2:15).

Are you ready to take hold of this eternal life? Are you ready for God to align your heart with his? Are you ready to grow in your knowledge of Jesus Christ? If so, get ready for the adventure of a lifetime. You will soon find that there is nothing better than knowing Jesus Christ. He is your life.

Rejoice. In Christ, you know the God of the universe. Even more amazing, the God of the universe knows you. And as Jesus said, this is eternal life.

Epilogue

Near the end of his life, Paul summoned the leaders of the church at Ephesus to meet him at Miletus. It would be their last time together. He let these leaders know that he was going to Jerusalem. Everyone knew this meant trouble for him—hardships and possible imprisonment. Yet he was compelled by the Spirit to go. And he was willing. As he wrote to the Philippians, "For to me, to live is Christ and to die is gain" (Philippians 1:21).

The grace of God was front and center in his conversation. His journey to Jerusalem was one more opportunity for him to carry out the task God had given him and equipped him to do. Nothing could keep him from going—not even danger. As he stated to these leaders, "I consider my life worth nothing to me; my only aim is to finish the race and complete the task the Lord Jesus has given me—the task of testifying to the good news of God's grace" (Acts 20:24).

Here, in one clear statement, Paul identifies the gospel in terms of God's grace. In essence, there is no good news apart from the grace of God. The simple gospel is simply grace.

God's grace was everything to Paul. And he wanted it to be everything to those he ministered to. He faced death and every kind of persecution for the sake of the gospel. This should say something to us. Far too many Christians look at grace as simply one in a long list of the doctrines of the faith. I think Paul would have some strong words to say to those who hold that view.

Grace as expressed in the new covenant is the overarching truth of the gospel. God has shown his favor to man in Jesus. Everything Jesus provided—life, forgiveness, justification, identity, his presence in us, and our freedom in him, to name a few—is a tangible expression of God's unmerited favor toward us.

The new life you have in Christ, the forgiveness you have in Christ, and the freedom you have in Christ are all gifts of grace, given freely and without conditions. His presence in you is grace. He freely chose to abide with you and to open the way for you to abide with him. The gospel is grace from start to finish.

As Paul was winding down his time at Miletus with the Ephesian leaders, he blessed them with these words: "Now I commit you to God and to the word of his grace, which can build you up and give you an inheritance among all those who are sanctified" (Acts 20:32).

My mom and dad spoke this word of grace to me when I moved to Dallas in 1982. Mom penned a letter expressing their heart toward me. Here are a few of her words: "We're so proud of you and so happy that you are letting God direct your life. Because of that we have no worries or fears. I just want you to know we support you in all that you do, and certainly have you in our prayers." I've read her letter hundreds of times through the years. I'm so grateful they pointed me to the grace of Jesus Christ.

My prayer is that this book has pointed you to Jesus Christ, to the wonders of his love and grace.

Nothing can award the heart true fulfillment, deep joy, or genuine contentment like the grace of God. His favor brings the purest and truest sense of happiness to the soul. Paul knew this. Wherever he went, he spoke that word and committed all to that word. Notice in all of his letters, the grace of Jesus Christ is the final note he strikes. This is what he wants you to know and experience.

Paul was not the only apostle, however, given the task of testifying to the grace of God. Peter concluded his first letter with these words: "I have written to you briefly, encouraging you and testifying that this is the true grace of God. Stand fast in it" (1 Peter 5:12). Can you think of a better place to stand than in God's unmerited favor? Can you think of a better place to be than in the person and work of Jesus Christ?

Peter's encouragement goes even further. We are not only to take our stand in the grace of God but also to grow in grace. Like Paul, Peter finishes his letter by striking the note of God's grace. This is what he wants to linger in our minds. This is what he wants to capture our hearts. The last sentence God's Spirit inspired Peter to write was this: "But grow in the grace and knowledge of our Lord and Savior Jesus Christ. To him be glory both now and forever! Amen" (2 Peter 3:18).

This isn't something Peter tacked on simply as a nice way to end the letter. Concerning the grace that has come to you, he said, "Even angels long to look into these things" (1 Peter 1:12). What you have in Jesus Christ has captured the attention of the angelic world. Wow! In the coming age, they will see the incomparable riches of God's grace in us.

> God raised us up with Christ and seated us with him in
> the heavenly realms in Christ Jesus, in order that in the
> coming ages he might show the incomparable riches of
> his grace, expressed in his kindness to us in Christ Jesus
> (Ephesians 2:6-7).

Grace is the way of salvation. Grace is the way of the Christian life. Grace will stand as an eternal testimony to all of creation.

As for you, grace opened the door to everything new. By faith in Jesus and his finished work, you've walked through. You've taken your stand. Now grow in grace and the knowledge of Jesus Christ. As Paul encouraged Timothy, "Fight the good fight of the faith. Take hold of the eternal life to which you were called" (1 Timothy 6:12). It's all yours in abundance by grace through faith.

The Bible begins with these words: "In the beginning God..."

It ends with these words: "The grace of the Lord Jesus be with God's people. Amen."

This is my prayer for you.

Notes

Introduction: God's Guy

1. C.S. Lewis, *Mere Christianity* (New York: Macmillan, 1952), p. 168.
2. Martyn Lloyd-Jones, *Spiritual Depression: Its Causes and Cure* (Grand Rapids, MI: Eerdmans, 1965), p. 132.

Chapter 7: From Fear to Faith

1. John Piper, "Why Do We Need to Be Born Again? Part 1" (sermon transcript), www.desiringgod.org, December 9, 2007.

Chapter 9: Let Go

1. Frederic Luskin, "The Art and Science of Forgiveness," *Stanford Medicine* 16, no. 4 (summer 1999), http://sm.stanford.edu/archive/stanmed/1999summer/forgiveness.html.

Chapter 10: Rest

1. Thomas Schreiner, "Penal Substitution View," in *The Nature of the Atonement: Four Views,* ed. James Beilby and Paul Eddy (Downers Grove, IL: InterVarsity Press, 2009), p. 67.

Chapter 11: You Are Free

1. Robert Farrar Capon, interview by Floyd Brown, *30 Good Minutes*, Chicago Sunday Evening Club, October 31, 1993. www.csec.org/index.php/archives/23-member-archives/700-robert-farrar-capon-program-3705.
2. Bureau of Justice Statistics, "3 in 4 Former Prisoners in 30 States Arrested Within 5 Years of Release," www.bjs.gov/content/pub/press/rprts05p0510pr.cfm.

Chapter 12: Don't Look Back

1. Seth Godin, "The Decline of Fascination and the Rise in Ennui," *Seth's Main Blog*, November 24, 2012, http://sethgodin.typepad.com/seths_blog/2012/11/the-decline-of-fascination-and-http://sethgodin.typepad.com.

Chapter 13: Living a Sunday Life in a Friday World

1. S.M. Lockridge, "It's Friday…but Sunday's Coming," audio recording of sermon, www.youtube.com/watch?v=8gx6_rGLz20.

Chapter 15: Eternal Life

1. Dan DeHaan, *The God You Can Know* (Chicago, Moody Press, 1982), p. 11.

2. N.T. Wright, *Justification: God's Plan and Paul's Vision* (Downers Grove, IL: InterVarsity Press, 2009), p. 238.

About Basic Gospel

Hear it. Believe it. Live it.

The gospel of Jesus Christ is simple, powerful, and life changing. It declares the love of God for mankind. It is the good news people long to hear. Radio delivers it straight to the heart.

But it is not enough just to hear the good news. God wants to make his love a reality in our lives. He wants us to believe it and live it.

At Basic Gospel, we are dedicated to proclaiming the name of Jesus Christ and the profound simplicity of his love and grace.

Our hope is that the clear presentation of the basic gospel and the singular focus on the death, burial, and resurrection of Jesus Christ will anchor listeners to the love of God and will encourage them to experience the fullness of the new-covenant life that is theirs in Christ.

Basic Gospel

751 Hebron Parkway, Suite 310
Lewisville, TX 75057

Office
214.890.4144

On-air line
844.32BASIC (844.322.2742)
toll-free from 4:00 p.m. to 4:25 p.m. Eastern Time

Order line
844.41BASIC (844.412.2742) toll-free

Visit our website at
www.basicgospel.net